The Mighty Marketer

Your Guide to Making More Money as a Freelance Medical Writer

Lori De Milto

Praise for *The Mighty Marketer:*
Your Guide to Making More Money
as a Freelance Medical Writer

"Are you an established, new or would-be freelance medical writer? Read The Mighty Marketer today! Successful medical writer Lori De Milto shares proven, practical steps to building your business in this engaging book that reads like a conversation with a trusted mentor."

— Genevieve J. Long, PhD
Freelance Medical Writer

"The Mighty Marketer is, in a word, fabulous! Lori has leveraged the lessons she learned from marketing her freelance business for more than two decades to write a clear, concise, easy-to-read marketing guide. I wish this book had been available when I launched my business!"

— Cynthia L. Kryder, MS, CCC-Sp
Medical Communications Specialist
Past President, American Medical Writers Association,
Delaware Valley Chapter
Author, "The Accidental Medical Writer"

"This book is compulsory reading if you're serious about launching, maintaining or growing a successful medical writing business. Lori shares practical insight based on experience and provides excellent tips and tools. You will learn from a masterful, mighty marketer!"

— Amy Rovi, Principal
Medivor, LLC

"The Mighty Marketer is just what the doctor ordered to help you plan and execute a marketing campaign for your medical writing business. When you are busy producing work for your clients, it is all too easy to neglect the essential task of generating new business. Lori's book will help you break through the inertia of thinking about marketing and get you to the point where you are actually doing it—and reaping the benefits."

— Nick Sidorovich, MSEd
Rolling Hill Media, LLC

"Being a great medical writer isn't enough if you're a freelancer. To be successful, you also need to be a great marketer. Ironically, while most of the freelancers I know want to be successful, very few are truly good at marketing. Many don't know what to do, and some simply don't want to do it.

Lori's 'can do' attitude, experience, and passion for helping other freelancers come through loud and clear in The Mighty Marketer. Lori IS The Mighty Marketer, and the stories, tips, and recommendations she provides in this book are perfect for those who are just starting out on the road to freelancing as well as for those who haven't achieved the level of success they desire because of a lack of marketing momentum.

The Mighty Marketer is a mighty great tool for kicking your freelance business into high gear!

— Brian Bass
Author, "The Accidental Medical Writer"
President, Bass Global, Inc.

"If the thought of 'selling' your writing abilities seems daunting, thoroughly read Lori De Milto's new book, The Mighty Marketer. Lori peppers her advice with personal experiences from her 20+ years as a successful medical writer to show you how easy it is to become a mighty marketer yourself. An enjoyable—and educational—read."

— Michelle Dalton, ELS
Founder, Dalton & Associates
Medical writing and editing specialists

"Lori has captured the essential tools needed for marketing a freelance medical writing business. This book is a must read for both new and seasoned medical writers who want to develop and market their business brand but don't know where to start."

— Ruwaida Vakil, MS
Owner ProMed Write LLC
Professional Medical Writing and Content Development
Services

The Mighty Marketer
Your Guide to Making More Money as a
Freelance Medical Writer

Lori De Milto

Published by BookLocker.com, Inc., Bradenton, Florida.

Printed in the United States of America on acid-free paper.

BookLocker.com, Inc.
2014

First Edition

DISCLAIMER

This book details the author's personal experiences with and opinions about marketing a freelance writing business. The author is not licensed in marketing.

The author and publisher are providing this book and its contents on an "as is" basis and make no representations or warranties of any kind with respect to this book or its contents. The author and publisher disclaim all such representations and warranties, including for example warranties of merchantability and marketing advice for a particular purpose. In addition, the author and publisher do not represent or warrant that the information accessible via this book is accurate, complete or current.

The statements made about products and services have not been evaluated by the U.S. government. Please consult with your own legal or accounting professional regarding the suggestions and recommendations made in this book.

Except as specifically stated in this book, neither the author or publisher, nor any authors, contributors, or other representatives will be liable for damages arising out of or in connection with the use of this book. This is a comprehensive limitation of liability that applies to all damages of any kind, including (without limitation) compensatory; direct, indirect or consequential damages; loss of data, income or profit; loss of or damage to property and claims of third parties.

You understand that this book is not intended as a substitute for consultation with a licensed legal or accounting professional. Before you begin any change your lifestyle in any way, you will consult a licensed professional to ensure that you are doing what's best for your situation.

This book provides content related to marketing topics. As such, use of this book implies your acceptance of this disclaimer.

DEDICATION

To my husband Julian De Milto, who has always believed in me.

Contents

Chapter 1. Building Your Business with Marketing Might

> "If you can dream it, you can do it."
> —Walt Disney

Within 18 months of starting my freelance medical writing business—with very little experience in medical writing—I had plenty of work and was earning twice as much as when I was a full-time writer for a major university. Since then, I've had as much work as I wanted, and usually more. The secret to my success is simple: mighty marketing.

No matter how talented a writer you are or how much you know about medicine, you won't succeed as a freelance medical writer unless you can market your services. Marketing is a key part of running a business. And freelance medical writing—or any type of freelance writing—is a business.

Control Your Destiny

Good marketing gives you the power to control your destiny—to decide how much you work, how much money you make, what type of work you do, and who you work for.

There are many definitions of marketing. Here are some that I like:

"Marketing is understanding your buyers really, really well. Then creating valuable products, services, and information especially for them to help solve their problems."
> —David Meerman Scott
> Bestselling author of "Real-Time Marketing and PR: How to Instantly Engage Your Market, Connect with Customers, and Create Products that Grow Your Business Now"

1

"Marketing is products that don't come back and consumers that do."
—Steve Dawson
President, Walkers Shortbread, Inc.

"Marketing is the science and art of exploring, creating, and delivering value to satisfy the needs of a target market at a profit."
—Philip Kotler, PhD
S.C. Johnson & Son Distinguished Professor
of International Marketing, Northwestern University
Kellogg Graduate School of Management

"Marketing is the art and science of creating, delighting and keeping customers, while making a profit and building enterprise value."
—Max Kalehoff
Vice President of Marketing, Clickable

"Marketing is discovering what the prospect wants and demands and delivering it more efficiently and effectively than the competition."
—Paul Kulavis
Managing Partner, Sterling Park Group

Become a Mighty Marketer

While minor revisions are necessary to make some of these definitions more relevant for freelance medical writers (we market services rather than products and have clients, not customers), marketing comes down to:

- Knowing what prospective clients (your target market) want and need
- Getting clients to hire you
- Keeping clients by giving them superior service.

Marketing your freelance medical writing business, in my view, covers virtually everything you do, from responding quickly and professionally to emails to having a great website to going beyond the expectations of your clients—and much more.

Yes, You Can

Marketing isn't difficult. If you're smart enough to be a freelance medical writer, you're smart enough to be a mighty marketer. Good marketing takes:

- Belief in the might of marketing
- Some basic marketing knowledge, which you can get through this book and the resources provided
- A can-do attitude
- A willingness to invest your time in work that is sometimes tedious
- A willingness to invest some money in marketing.

Freelance medical writers sometimes think "marketing" is a dirty word or something to be ashamed of doing. It's not. It's a sound, and necessary, business practice.

Exploring potential opportunities and clients should be fun. I could easily spend much more time marketing my business than I do. Once you put on your marketer's hat, the ideas will start to flow. The keys are to set your priorities and stick to them, and to spend enough time on marketing to grow your business but not so much that you don't have time to do the work.

Enjoying the Marketing Journey

A strong belief in the might of marketing, some basic knowledge, a "can-do" attitude, and lots of hard work let me successfully market my business. This book tells you how I did it—and how you can too.

My personal experiences, the many things I've learned over the years from colleagues, and insights from many credible books and Web-based resources (associations, organizations and individuals) are included. While some of the content is specific to medical writing, you can apply most of it to any type of freelance writing business.

The worksheets, templates and tools in Bonus #2 will make it easy for you to focus your marketing and make the best use of your time and money.

Chapter 2. Learning From My Journey as a Mighty Marketer

"I am a great believer in luck.
The harder I work, the more I have of it."
— Thomas Jefferson

I started freelancing in 1990. Back then, it was a way for me to explore future career opportunities. I knew that I had learned and earned as much as I could in my job as a communications manager, essentially a one-person communications department, for the business school of a major university. As I started freelancing, I found that I really liked it, was good at it, and wanted to do it full time.

How I Became a Medical Writer Without Really Trying

Through my early marketing efforts, including direct mail and networking, I starting getting medical editing and writing assignments—without focusing on the field or knowing much about health and medicine. My first steady gig in medical editing gave me a source of income when I launched my freelance writing business full time a few years later.

How I got this work shows something I firmly believe—anything you do and anyone you meet can lead to a business opportunity in the future. Through my work at the university, I learned about a graduate of an executive program who had bought into a printing company. I sent him a letter congratulating him on his new venture and asked him to keep me in mind if he ever needed freelance writing or editing services. He called me and asked me to do some proofreading for him, becoming one of my first clients.

> **TIP:**
> Consider everything you do and anyone you meet a possible business opportunity.

The work, mostly proofreading an internal newsletter for a supermarket, was boring. The turnaround was tight. When I left work, I had to stop by his office to pick up the job (this was in the days before email) and I had to turn in the completed job on my way to the office the next day. The pay was low.

Saying Yes when Opportunity Knocks

One day, my client called and asked if I would be interested in copyediting a journal on drug and device development. A client of his, a nonprofit association for professionals working in medical product development, was looking for a good copyeditor. Based on the work I had done for him, he said he'd be happy to recommend me.

Although I've always considered myself a writer and was much more interested in writing than copyediting, I said yes. As a budding freelancer, I knew that I needed to be open to anything that would help me learn. So my client introduced me to his client, and I spent the next 10 years copyediting the journal, eventually also doing some writing for the association. I had a steady income, which gave me financial confidence when I launched my freelance business full time. And I learned a lot about medical product development, a key part of medical writing.

During this period, I also did some writing for a major university hospital's newsletter for referring physicians. I landed this client through networking. After letting people in my network know that I was available for freelance assignments, a colleague from a professional association introduced me to her neighbor, who did communications for the university hospital and hired freelance writers for the newsletter.

From Part-Time to Full-Time Freelance Medical Writer

After I had dabbled as a freelancer for about a year, I began making plans to transition into full-time freelancing. At that point, I had 2 1/2 years before I would be vested in my university's retirement plan. I decided to launch my full-time freelance business shortly after I was vested in early 1997 and spend the time until then marketing and building my business. I took on more freelance work so I'd have a steadier income when I finally took the plunge. The next few years, while I was working full-time for the university and doing as much freelance work as I could handle, were hectic.

Launching my full-time freelance writing business was a lot of fun. Since I was so well prepared, and had one fairly large steady client, it was only a little scary. I admit, though, that I did a lot of things by instinct in the early days, backed by a little knowledge (mostly from reading books on marketing, direct mail and running a business). A book like this would have been very helpful to me back then. Fortunately, my instincts were good and my focus on marketing enabled me to quickly grow my business.

Marketing My Business Early and Aggressively

From the start, I treated freelancing as the business that it is, investing the time and money necessary to succeed. I developed a business name, a tagline, and a logo, and used them in professional marketing materials: business cards, brochure, envelopes, and direct mail pieces (at the time, the Web was in its infancy, and even large organizations were just starting to develop websites). As a journalism major and marketing communications writer, I had the expertise to write my own copy. But I hired a professional graphic designer to design and produce my marketing materials.

7

> **TIP:**
> Invest time and money in marketing your freelance medical writing business.

I learned about and joined the American Medical Writers Association, or AMWA, one of the best things any freelance medical writer can do. I went to the annual conference, got actively involved with my chapter and listed my services in AMWA's Freelance Directory.

The mailing lists for my early direct mail campaigns were the product of many hours of research. I starting by searching the AMWA Member Directory for companies I might want to work for and contacts in those companies. Then I went to the library to search directories of hospitals, healthcare associations and other healthcare organizations for more potential clients. Today, you can easily do this kind of research on the Web.

Investing in Marketing Pays Off

In my first 18 months as a full-time freelance medical writer, I sent three direct mail flyers to about 250 people each, spending about $7,000. My total marketing costs were about $10,000.

Don't stop reading. This was the foundation of my success. It was worth every penny.

But you don't have to spend nearly as much as I did to be a good marketer. The Web was in its infancy at the time, and LinkedIn didn't exist. These technological advances let you market well now at much less expense.

My direct mail campaign produced as much business as I wanted. Some clients contacted me within days of receiving the first flyer. Others hired me after receiving the second or third flyer. I realized that it was important to continually market my business so that potential clients would remember me when they needed help. One client hired me nearly two years after I sent him the first flyer—and I've been working with him ever since.

I also found freelance opportunities through AMWA. Along with using the Member Directory to develop lists for my direct mail campaign, I found work through the jobs list (now called Jobs Online but produced in print back then) and the AMWA Freelance Directory. As I built my experience and became more involved with AMWA, I began to get referrals for work.

Using the Web for Marketing

In 2002, as the Web was starting to grow, I created a website for my business. At the time, few writers had websites. Mine was pretty basic in its design and content but it was clean and professional. It gave potential clients the information they needed to see whether I might be the right writer for them.

I revised my website (writerforrent.net) in 2008, adding more content and hiring a professional Web designer. Getting the content just right took many hours of research and writing. My research included looking at every website of freelance writers listed in AMWA's Freelance Directory. My new design was expensive, but based on positive feedback from clients and colleagues, well worth it. I revised my website again in 2014, shortening the content and using an updated design, implemented by a professional Web designer.

I was also an early adopter of social networking, getting started before most people had even heard of the term. When a colleague invited me to join her LinkedIn network in 2004, I didn't really know what it was. But I figured it couldn't hurt, and accepted her invitation. Since then, LinkedIn has grown to become the most important social network for business. I've gotten business through LinkedIn and know other freelance writers who have too.

New Opportunities Through Marketing

My freelance writing business hasn't been all smooth sailing. Through consistent, assertive marketing and giving my clients targeted copy and content, on time, every time, I've avoided the feast or famine syndrome that afflicts many freelance writers. In fact, most of my freelance work life has been a continual feast.

But bad things have happened. I lost a lot of work in 2001, because a client had to cancel an annual conference scheduled for a few days after the terrorist attack. I would have written about 40 articles based on that conference. Another time, I resigned from doing lots of work I loved for a client I loved because of quality and ethical issues with a new staff member I had to work with. I did try to resolve these issues, but was unable to do so.

When a very prestigious hospital hired me for a large Web writing project, I was thrilled. Things went well until they hired a new marketing manager for the therapeutic area I was working in. She wanted a much more detailed website than had been specified in the contract. I said that I would be glad to write the more detailed website but that it would involve significantly more time and thus, cost. The project manager, who had little experience in her job, told me to follow the original project scope, as per the contract. Was it any surprise that the new marketing manager didn't like my work?

Had this been a long-term client, the project manager and her bosses in the marketing department would have known that I had done the job well as instructed. The project manager would have told the marketing manager that I had done what I had been asked to do. We probably would have continued to work together. Since it was my first project for the client, they didn't know the quality of my work and I was blamed when the new marketing manager was unhappy with the website.

TIP:
When bad things happen, turn them into new opportunities through marketing.

No matter how good you are, things will happen. I've found, though, that when one door closes, another opens, usually within a few months—as long as you give it a little push with marketing. Satisfied clients and colleagues often refer me to potential clients.

The push here is the good work I've done in the past (satisfied clients) or my good reputation (colleagues). When I'm actively looking for work, which is rare these days, I kick the marketing up a notch. Usually, I do a targeted direct mail campaign, focused on the type of clients I'd most like to work with. And I let my clients and colleagues know that I'm available for interesting assignments. Most of the time, I've ended up doing more interesting work or new types of work.

Seeds of Success

Over time, I came to think of marketing as planting seeds. Not every seed in a garden will grow, and some take longer than others to rise from the earth, but with consistent watering and care, the result is a garden full of many beautiful flowers. Every marketing contact or tactic hasn't brought in new clients, but with consistent, high-quality efforts, and a willingness to invest my time and money, my freelance medical writing business has bloomed profusely.

Making Your Own Luck

If you've got the skills and talent to be a medical writer and are willing to work hard, you too can use marketing to succeed as a freelance medical writer.* In many ways, it's much easier to do this today than it was when I started. The Web gives you easy access to many marketing and medical writing resources, social media venues, and ways to research potential clients.

---

* Are You Ready to Be a Freelance Medical Writer?

Before you launch a freelance business, make sure you're ready. Have you:

- Worked as a medical writer for a company?
- Done some writing while working as a medical professional or scientist?

- Worked as a writer outside of health and medicine?

If you answered "no" to all of these questions, it will be very difficult for you to succeed as a freelance medical writer and impossible for you to become a mighty marketer right now. Get some relevant experience and then launch a freelance business.

Resources

BOOK

Brian G. Bass and Cynthia L. Kryder, "The Accidental Medical Writer," 2008. www.theaccidentalmedicalwriter.com

Chapter 3. Understanding the Freelance Medical Writing Marketplace

"The ladder of success is best climbed by stepping
on the rungs of opportunity."
— Ayn Rand

Opportunities for interesting and lucrative work abound in the freelance medical writing marketplace. You can do many types of work for many types of clients. The first step on your marketing journey is to learn about both the opportunities and the clients (called market research).

Explore Your Options Through Market Research

Fortunately, it's easy to learn about the freelance medical writing marketplace now, and well worth the time it takes to do this. When I was starting out, I thought that all medical writers were like me: people with journalism or English degrees who did marketing communications in the fields of health and medicine. It was quite a shock when I attended my first AMWA annual conference and learned that most medical writers have scientific or medical degrees and write what I call high science: journal articles, slide decks, regulatory writing, etc.

TIP
Join AMWA now. If you're already a member, volunteer so people get to know you.

Web-based and Face-to-Face Market Research

AMWA provides many ways to do Web-based and face-to-face market research. Web resources include the Toolkit for New Medical Writers, which lists types of medical writing freelance medical writers do and the types of clients they work for, and the AMWA Freelance Directory, which has profiles of freelance medical writers you can read to see what they do (and how they market themselves).

Learn About the Marketplace Through AMWA

Some Web-based resources:

- Toolkit for New Medical Writers
- Freelance Directory

Face-to-face networking with other freelance medical writers and potential clients:

- AMWA annual conference
- AMWA Delaware Valley Chapter freelance conference
- Other AMWA chapter meetings and conferences

Virtual networking:

- AMWA LinkedIn groups
- AMWA community forums

Learn more about freelance medical writing by chatting with AMWA members—freelance medical writers and potential clients—about what they do and who they work for. You'll meet many freelance medical writers and some people who hire us at the AMWA annual conference, held each fall in different cities throughout the United States. The annual conference includes some sessions just for freelancers where you can learn more about the field and network with others. If your chapter has meetings and events, you can also do market research by attending these.

Every spring, my AMWA chapter, Delaware Valley, hosts a full-day freelance conference in Pennsylvania, attracting about 80 freelance medical writers. It's a great opportunity to network with other freelancers and learn more about the field. The program brochure is posted on the chapter's website (www.amwa-dvc.org) a few months before the event each year.

You can also network virtually through AMWA's community forums and LinkedIn group, as well as other LinkedIn groups related to freelance writing, writing, healthcare, medical marketing, and more. Find other information about medical writing through your own Web searches and by joining organizations like the National Association of Science Writers and the Drug Information Association's Medical Writing Special Interest Area Community.

Start Your Prospect Lists

As you do your market research, start making lists of:

- Types of clients you'd like to work with
- Specific organizations you'd like to work with
- Therapeutic areas you'd like to work in.

Put an asterisk next to any clients, organizations or therapeutic areas that you're especially interested in.

Also see the worksheet for defining your services, therapeutic areas and clients in Bonus #2: Mighty Marketing Worksheets, Templates and Tools.

Learn How to Market to Other Businesses

Marketing your freelance writing business is very different than marketing something that millions of consumers buy every week in supermarkets, like milk or bread. That's actually good, because it's far less complicated and much more affordable to market freelance medical writing services than milk or bread.

You'll be marketing your freelance medical writing services to businesses and other organizations, such as non-profit organizations, government agencies and universities. Marketing to these organizations is called business-to-business, or B2B, marketing.

How B2B Marketing is Different

Compared to marketing to consumers, the B2B market is:

- Much smaller and more targeted
- Driven by personal relationships
- Focused on company image, brand and reputation.

It also has a longer marketing cycle.

Your market research will help you match your interests, experience and capabilities with your target clients. Then you can do more research to learn about specific types of clients. For example, I like to write for hospitals. So I developed a list of hospitals and then visited their websites to read their Web content, newsletters and other publications. This market research will guide your marketing plan.

Learn more in Planning for Your Success (Chapter 5).

A Longer Marketing Cycle

While it may seem like clients always need to find freelance medical writers fast, in general, it takes time to land clients, especially the kind of clients you'll want to work with over the long term. The marketing cycle — how long it takes to land clients — is longer for B2B than for mass-market consumer products. It includes the time needed to build awareness of your brand and your services. A good brand will help you get noticed and set you apart from the competition.

Learn more in Creating Your Brand (Chapter 4).

What Clients Want

Clients of freelance medical writers have a strong interest in our services. They need our help to succeed. Excellent writing skills are a prerequisite. Other requirements, even for the same type of client for the same type of work, may vary. But in general, clients want:

- Experience in medical writing, the therapeutic area, and the type of writing
- Specific degree(s)
- Ability to meet deadlines (the key to repeat business)
- Excellent communication skills
- Flexibility, accessibility and responsiveness
- Ability to take ownership of the project.

Clients want freelance writers they can depend on and work with long term. I've been working with one of my largest clients for 17 years and another for 16 years (as of 2014). I make their professional lives easier and function as an extension of their internal team.

Understanding the freelance medical writing marketplace will help you target and market your services appropriately and build win-win relationships with clients.

Resources

AMERICAN MEDICAL WRITERS ASSOCIATION

American Medical Writers Association (National organization)
www.amwa.org (Some information is only available to members)

Toolkit for New Medical Writers: Includes an overview of medical writing, including types of employers and types of work, with a section on freelance medical writing.

Freelance Directory: Learn more about what other freelance medical writers do and how they market themselves.

About Medical Communication: Resources about medical communication, including a PowerPoint presentation.

Education tab: Annual conference information.

AMWA-Delaware Valley Chapter
(www.amwa-dvc.org)

Upcoming Events: Where freelance conference information will be posted.

Delawriter newsletter, with articles about many aspects of medical writing and presentations at past freelance conferences.

LINKED IN GROUPS

American Medical Writers Association (not limited to freelancers but still useful)

Freelancers in Medical Communications

Healthcare Marketing, Communications and Education Professionals

Many others

E-NEWSLETTERS

SmartBrief
www.smartbrief.com
More than 40 e-newsletters in health care, including one for health care marketers

Chapter 4. Creating Your Brand

"If you are not a brand, you are a commodity."
— Philip Kotler

A good brand creates a positive and lasting impression in the minds of your prospects and colleagues. A bad brand—or not having a brand—means they're likely to quickly forget you. The American Marketing Association defines a brand as "A name, term, design, symbol, or any other feature that identifies one seller's good or service as distinct from those of other sellers."

Let's say that all freelance medical writers are competent writers and knowledgeable about medicine. The things that make us somewhat different from each other are:

- Our education (science, medicine, pharmacy, journalism, English, etc.)
- The type of work we do (e.g., journal articles and slide decks versus hospital website content and magazines for consumers)
- Our therapeutic areas of expertise.

But many freelance medical writers have the same or similar degrees and areas of expertise, and do the same or similar types of work. So these things can be part of your brand, but they're not enough.

Rise Above the Crowd

What will make you rise above the crowd is the way you position yourself as being able to solve clients' problems and meet their needs—in your brand. I know that doing the job right and getting it done on time are very important to clients. So my branding focuses on delivering what they need (targeted copy and content) when they need it (on time, every time). I've carried this concept through in my logo, business card, website (writerforrent.net) and all my marketing materials. I also chose a company name, Lori De Milto Writer for Rent, that's memorable and instantly tells people what I do. Your brand doesn't need to be as glitzy as mine, but you do need to have one.

What's in a Brand?

Everything in your brand needs to work together. If this all seems overwhelming, don't worry. Once you define your brand, you can—and should—hire a graphic designer to implement it. I did, and even though I had some basic design skills and a desktop publishing program, my designer did a much better job than I ever could have.

Elements of a Brand

- Company name
- Logo: A symbol or other design to identify an organization's services
- Tagline: A memorable phrase or sentence that captures the essence of your brand
- Print and Web design: Colors, fonts, tone, etc., to be used in all marketing materials
- Key messages: From your brand and beyond

You'll need a professional headshot too. While not technically part of your brand, it's an important part of your image. You'll need this for your website, LinkedIn profile, speaking engagements, etc.

Create a Mighty Brand

Creating your brand will actually help you market your freelance medical writing services, because it will force you to think about what you want to do and what you can offer clients.

Your Role in the Freelance Medical Writing Marketplace

Freelance medical writers do many types of work for many types of clients. Use your market research to start to figure out what you want to do, what you can do and what clients will hire you to do. While your skills, education, professional experience and interests all influence where you fit in the medical writing marketplace, strong branding and marketing can open new and sometimes unexpected doors.

> **TIP:**
> Review AMWA freelance directory listings and make a list of interesting work other freelancers are doing.

Consider What Clients Need and How You Can Meet Those Needs

Consider what clients generally look for in a freelance medical writer: someone with the right experience and (usually) education who is flexible and responsive and can get the job done on time while making life easier for them. To learn what's most important to specific prospective clients or types of clients, visit the websites of some of the companies you'd like to work with. See how they describe themselves and the qualities they value. Take notes.

Now consider how you can meet the needs of these clients or types of clients. Take notes about your important qualities that are important to them, based on what you've learned about the freelance medical writing marketplace and these types of clients or specific organizations.

Consider the Brands of Other Freelance Medical Writers

Study the brands of other freelance medical writers. Start with AMWA's freelance directory. Read the listings. Visit the websites of other freelance medical writers to see how they brand and market themselves. Also read their LinkedIn profiles. Doing this will spark great ideas, but don't plagiarize their brands.

Make notes about what you like and don't like. Consider each brand's:

- Tone (e.g., bold, conservative or intellectual)
- Logos and taglines
- Language
- Colors
- Other graphics.

Put it All Together in Your Brand

Review your market research, what type of work you'd like to do, who you'd like to work with and how other freelance medical writers brand themselves. Looking at all of this together should spark ideas.

Make notes about things you might want to use in your brand, such as words to describe yourself or colors that you like. Then put this aside and go on to other things. Think about it now and then over the next few days, and you'll come up with more ideas. Your best brand ideas will probably come when you're not even thinking about this!

Define Your Brand

Describe:

- What you offer
- Who you offer it to (type of clients)
- How your services are different and better—or can be positioned as different and better
- The promise(s) you're making to clients

How you position yourself in the freelance medical writing marketplace, and the promises you make—and keep—through your branding will set you apart from the competition. Think about Coca-Cola and Pepsi. Coca-Cola was #3 on Forbes Magazine's 2013 list of the world's most valuable brands. Pepsi, a nearly identical product, was #25. That's the power of branding.

Not everything in your description will become part of your brand, but you need to know these things to develop a good brand (and to develop your marketing plan, covered in the next chapter). Play around with some taglines. An easy way to do this is to take the words and qualities that you think are important and start arranging them in different ways.

Also consider the tone of your brand, which covers both the language you use and your design. I do medical marketing communications and love to write Web content. So I developed a bold, conversational brand that appeals to my target clients. If I were a scientific medical writer and wanted to work with pharmaceutical companies, I would have developed a more conservative brand.

At this point, your ideas about what you want to say and how you want to say it don't have to be perfect, and you don't have to know exactly how you'd like your brand to look. When you're reasonably happy with your brand-to-be, get feedback from other freelance medical writers whose marketing you respect, and other people you know in the field. Turn to people outside of medical writing too, especially anyone who works in marketing, loves to read or just seems like they could help.

When you're ready to begin implementing your brand, a good designer can develop a logo and other graphics that reflect your language, key messages and tone.

Use Your Brand to Make the Right Impression

Putting your brand to work for you is the fun part. Use your brand on all of your marketing materials, even things you may not think of as marketing materials, like your email signature. Some marketing materials, like your business card and your website, will display your full brand: logo, tagline, colors, etc. Others, like your email signature, may only contain part of your brand.

My brand is very recognizable and has brought me many compliments from clients and colleagues. People generally remember me because of my strong and distinct brand.

Resources

ARTICLES

John Williams, "The Basics of Branding," Entrepreneur. www.entrepreneur.com/article/77408# (Accessed 3/28/14)

"How to Develop a Brand." www.dummies.com/how-to/content/how-to-develop-a-brand.html (Accessed 3/28/14)

BOOK

Catriona Mackay, "Effective Marketing in Easy Steps," Easy Steps Limited, 2011.

Chapter 5. Planning for Your Success

"Failing to plan is planning to fail."
— Alan Lakein

A good marketing plan is the key to marketing your freelance medical writing business effectively and efficiently. This can be as simple as a few pages of notes, lists, action items, and deadlines. But those few pages can make the difference between success and failure. Developing your marketing plan will give you a better understanding of potential and current clients and a list of actions to take to help you get (and keep) clients.

Benefits of a Good Marketing Plan

- Learn more about opportunities
- Use your limited resources—time and money—efficiently
- Market your business with ease

Your marketing plan should cover the next 12 months in some detail. Ideally, it should also lay out your general marketing goal for the next two to five years.

Six Easy Steps to Your Marketing Plan

Follow these six easy steps, and you'll have a marketing plan:

1. Define what you offer
2. Identify your target market
3. Set your goal
4. Choose your tactics
5. State your actions
6. Set aside a budget.

Steps one and two are nearly complete if you've already done your market research (covered in Chapter 3) and your branding (covered in Chapter 4).

> **TIP:**
> Use Mighty Marketing Worksheets, Templates and Tools (Bonus #2) to easily focus your marketing.

Define What You Offer

Take your market research about the medical writing marketplace and decide what you plan to offer clients. Develop lists of your services and therapeutic areas of expertise.

Services and Therapeutic Areas of Expertise

#1 Priority Services and Therapeutic Areas:
- Types of medical writing you currently do or have done and want to pursue
- Therapeutic areas you've worked in and want to pursue

#2 Priority Services and Therapeutic Areas:
- Types of medical writing you do or have done but do not want to pursue
- Therapeutic areas you've worked in and do not want to pursue

#3 Priority Services and Therapeutic Areas:
- Types of medical writing you haven't done but really want to do
- Therapeutic areas you haven't worked in but really want to work in

Define what you'll charge for your services. See the AMWA salary survey (available to AMWA members at www.amwa.org)

and talk to colleagues about what they charge for various types of writing and clients. Factor in your experience level.

Identify Your Target Market

Also use your market research to define your target market and start developing general prospect lists. Remember, if you're not yet established, think broadly. As you become more established, you can begin to target your markets more narrowly.

When I started out, I just had a general list of associations, pharmaceutical companies, medical communication companies, hospitals, and so forth. As I gained experience and learned more about the marketplace and what I wanted to do, I developed specific target markets like National Cancer Institute cancer centers and academic medical centers.

General Prospect Lists

#1 Priority Clients:
- The type of clients you've worked with and would like to pursue
- Any specific clients you'd like to work with

#2 Priority Clients:
- The type of clients you've worked with but do not want to pursue
- Any specific clients you would like to work with (even though you're not generally interested in this type of client)

#3 Priority Clients:
- Type of clients you haven't worked with but really want to work with
- Any specific clients you'd like to work with

Set Your Goal

Now that you know what you'll offer and who you'd like to work with, you're ready to set your goal. A goal is a specific result that you need to achieve to be a successful freelance medical writer. Sample goals are:

Increase revenue by 25 percent over the next 12 months (by month, year) OR

Expand into two new types of medical writing over the next 12 months (by month, year) OR

Increase repeat business from current clients by 20 percent over the next 12 months (by month, year).

Be Realistic

Set a goal that you will make you work hard, but that you can achieve. Make it easy to measure and include a target date for achieving the goal.

The more established you are in medical writing, the more specific you can be about your goal. The newer you are, the wider the net you'll need to cast. When I was starting out, I took work I'd never consider today, like writing entries for a health encyclopedia. But I wanted to learn more about medical writing and build my portfolio. My initial goal was:

Build my freelance writing business by 50 percent in the first year and learn more about medical writing while providing great service to clients.

Today, I can pick and choose the work that I do. My current goal reflects this:

Provide targeted medical marketing copy and content to current clients while increasing revenue 10 percent in the next year. Pursue new opportunities only when the work and client excite me.

If you find that your goal isn't realistic, that's okay. Change it to something you can achieve.

Also see the worksheet for setting your marketing goals in Bonus #2: Mighty Marketing Worksheets, Templates and Tools.

Choose Your Tactics

Tactics, or tools, are the practical things you'll use to achieve your goal. Essential tools for freelance medical writers are:

- Elevator pitch
- Business card and email signature
- LinkedIn
- AMWA freelance directory
- Networking
- Website.

If you absolutely can't afford to develop your website right away, make this your #1 priority for year two.

Effective tools for freelance medical writers—which will improve your marketing results but aren't absolutely necessary—include:

- Direct mail
- Email marketing
- Cards and gifts
- Printed marketing materials.

Also see the worksheet for choosing your tools in Bonus #2: Mighty Marketing Worksheets, Templates and Tools.

Read More About Essential and Effective Tools

Read more about essential and effective tools, and how to develop them, in these chapters:

- Making Marketing Work for You: Parts 1 and 2 (Chapters 6 and 9)
- Making a Name for Yourself: Networking and Reputation Building (Chapter 7)
- Creating a Compelling Website (Chapter 8).

State Your Actions

Mighty marketing keeps you in the minds of clients and colleagues when they need a freelance medical writer or know someone who does. It requires deliberate and frequent contact. Sometimes you'll be doing active marketing, like a direct mail or email campaign. You should always be doing marketing activities like networking.

TIP:
Keep your marketing on track with a calendar of marketing actions and deadlines.

State the actions you'll take to achieve your marketing goals in an annual marketing calendar. Include a deadline for each action. Also include the cost of each action, which is an easy way to track your marketing expenses (as distinct from other business expenses).

You can do the calendar by month or quarter. When you launch your business or first rev up your marketing efforts, expect to spend much more time on marketing than in later years.

Also see the worksheet for the annual marketing calendar in Bonus #2: Mighty Marketing Worksheets, Templates and Tools.

Sample Marketing Calendar: Year #1, Month #1

Every Friday: Review marketing actions

Action item #1: Develop elevator pitch
Deadline:
Date completed:
Cost: None

Action item #2: Develop initial business card and get it printed
Deadline:

Date completed:
Cost:

Action item #3: Develop email signature
Deadline:
Date completed:
Cost: None

Action item #4: Develop and post LinkedIn profile
Deadline:
Date completed:
Cost: None

Action item #5: Develop and post AMWA freelance
directory profile
Deadline:
Date completed:
Cost:

Set Aside a Budget

Budget for your marketing expenses. While some marketing tactics, like LinkedIn and your elevator pitch, are free, most cost money. Like any business, you need to spend money to make money as a freelance medical writer. Fortunately, some high-impact marketing tools, like a business card, don't cost much.

But, you must invest in high-quality design (print and Web) and high-quality marketing materials. If you don't, you won't look like—or be treated as—a professional.

For the first year in business, or the first year you rev up your marketing, I'd recommend about $5,000-$8,000 if you develop your website and attend the AMWA annual conference and about $2,000 if you do neither of these things. If you don't develop your website until the next year, budget for it then (roughly $1,000-$3,000).

Some costs are fixed or standard, such as AMWA membership, AMWA Freelance Directory, and annual conference;

and printing business cards and other marketing materials. Other costs, such as design services (print and web), vary by geographic region and vendor. Estimated costs are as of 2014.

Put Your Plan into Action

> **TIP:**
> Set aside a regular time every week for marketing, and take action item deadlines seriously.

Now that you have an easy-to-follow marketing plan, you need to take the actions that will help you achieve your goal. It's easy to let marketing slip through the cracks, but very important not to do this. Set aside a regular time to work on your marketing, such as every Friday afternoon or Tuesday and Thursday evenings. Complete your action items as if each were a deadline for a client.

Be Flexible

Be flexible. As things around you change and you learn more about the freelance medical writing marketplace from your experiences and networking, you'll need to revise your marketing plan and your tools.

Review and Update Your Plan

Review your marketing plan every quarter and update it as needed. Make notes about what works and doesn't work for you. Update your plan in the last quarter of each year for the next year.

Resources

BOOKS

Robert Bly, "Marketing Plan Handbook," Entrepreneur Media, 2009.

Jay Conrad Levinson and Jeannie Levinson. "Guerrilla Marketing Field Guide: 30 Powerful Maneuvers for Non-Stop Momentum and Results," Entrepreneur Press, 2013.

Catriona Mackay, "Effective Marketing in Easy Steps," Easy Steps Limited, 2011.

WEBSITES

Guerilla Marketing
www.gmarketing.com

Entrepreneur.com
www.entrepreneur.com/marketing/index.html#

Marketing Zone
www.marketingzone.com/how

ASSOCIATION

AMWA
www.AMWA.org

Chapter 6. Making Marketing Work for You (Part 1): Essential Marketing Tools

"The best way to predict the future is to create it."
— Peter Drucker

With the right tools, marketing your freelance writing business will be easy. There are essential marketing tools—which you must have—and effective marketing tools—which you can use.

Fortunately, some of the best marketing tools for freelance medical writers are free or low cost. Develop the essential marketing tools before you launch your business or as soon after that as possible. You can put most of these tools to work for you in a few days.

Also see Making Marketing Work for You (Part 2): Effective Marketing Tools (Chapter 9).

Essential Marketing Tools

- Elevator pitch
- Business card and email signature
- LinkedIn
- AMWA Freelance Directory
- Networking
- Website

Create a Mighty First Impression

When you meet people in person for the first time, your elevator pitch and business card are key tools for creating a positive first impression. Your email signature will help you promote your business using today's most common form of business communication.

Your Elevator Pitch

What will you say so that people understand—in 60 seconds or less—what you do? Your elevator pitch (also called an elevator speech) should cover what you can do for clients and how you can solve their problems (the benefits or results of your work). It should leave the person you're talking to wanting to know more about you and your services.

Think about your elevator pitch before you head out the door or pick up the phone. Write down your ideas and say them aloud to see how they sound. Refine your ideas until you've got a concise, compelling way to introduce yourself. If you've already developed your brand (Chapter 4), you're close to having an elevator pitch. If you haven't developed your brand yet, you can refine your elevator pitch after doing that. Practice your elevator pitch, because using it won't feel natural.

My elevator pitch is:

> "I help clients communicate clearly with their target audiences—consumers, patients, physiccians, and others—through targeted medical marketing copy and content. I specialize in writing newsletters, magazines and Web content for hospitals."

Your Business Card

A great business card is a small but powerful ad for your business. Done right, it will help potential clients and colleagues remember you, especially when they get back to the office with a stack of business cards.

Done wrong, it will mark you as unprofessional, as will not having a business card at all. I've met many freelance medical writers in professional networking situations who didn't have business cards. I rarely remember these people, and I certainly wouldn't rank them highly as people to cultivate as part of my network.

Attributes of a Great Business Card

- Clear, concise information
- Clean, legible, professional design
- Branded
- Professionally printed

Information to include:

- Your name
- Company name (if you have one now)
- Tagline (if you have one now)
- Brief description of your services (if you don't have a tagline and your company name doesn't clearly say what you do)
- Logo (if you have one now)
- Business phone number
- Email address
- Website (if you have one now)

Optional information to include:

- Mailing address
- LinkedIn address

Design and Printing

Your business card design should be clean and simple so people can easily see who you are, what you do and how to contact you. Make the key information most prominent. On my card, my company name, logo and tagline have the most space. My phone number, email address and website are easily seen in the top right part of my business card. But my address, the least important information, is separate and at the bottom of the card.

If you're just starting out and on a tight budget, or need business cards before you've established your brand and hired a designer to create your look, try templates through web-based services like Vistaprint (vistaprint.com) or Staples (Staples.com) to design and print your business cards professionally at very reasonable prices. If you've already had your business card professionally designed, you can upload it to these services for printing.

> **TIP**
> Always carry a few business cards. You could meet a potential client or contact anywhere at any time.

Email Signature

Your email signature is a mighty, but often neglected, marketing tool. Include:

- Your name
- Company name (if you have one now)
- Tagline (if you have one now)
- Logo (if you have one now)
- Business phone number
- Website (if you have one now)
- LinkedIn address
- Mailing address (optional).

If your company name doesn't clearly explain what you do, or you don't have a tagline that does this, include a very brief description of your services (less than a sentence).

Persuade Your Target Audience: LinkedIn and AMWA Freelance Directory

LinkedIn and the AMWA Freelance Directory can be great marketing tools—if you invest the time in crafting persuasive profiles. With 250 million members as of April 2014, LinkedIn is the world's largest professional network. "When you join LinkedIn, you get access to people, jobs, news, updates, and insights that help you be great at what you do," says the company's website.

Adds LinkedIn guru Donna Serdula, "Your LinkedIn profile is your career future." Serdula spoke at the 2014 AMWA Delaware Valley Chapter freelance conference.

Clients can search the AWMA Freelance Directory for free. At $75 a year for an ad (in 2014), it's a real bargain for freelance medical writers. I've covered LinkedIn first because you can be proactive on LinkedIn and seek out opportunities, whereas with the AMWA Freelance Directory, clients have to find you.

Crafting Persuasive Profiles

Write to your target audience and focus on the benefits you provide in both your LinkedIn and AMWA Freelance Directory profiles. Much of the content will be the same. (AMWA calls entries in the Freelance Directory "listings," but I've used the term "profile" here to keep things simple.)

Elements of Persuasive Profiles

Content:
- Scintillating summary or description with an enticing headline or first sentence, benefits to your target audience, and clear, simple description of who you are and what you do
- Key branding messages
- Summary of experience, services and therapeutic areas
- More details on experience
- Education
- Relevant honors and awards
- Clear call to action (e.g., call or email, visit my website, connect on LinkedIn, or any combination of these)

- Five strategic keywords or phrases used throughout your profile
- Links to your website, writing samples or both

Format:
- Headlines and subheads
- Short, action-oriented sentences
- Short paragraphs
- Bulleted lists

Use key messages from your branding work, your elevator pitch and your services and therapeutic areas to craft your profiles. If you've developed your website, or at least the content for your website, you'll have most (maybe all) of the information you'll need.

> **TIP:**
> Study LinkedIn and Freelance Directory profiles of other freelance writers for good ideas.

There are some differences in the formats of LinkedIn and the AMWA Freelance Directory that affect what you'll say and how your profiles will look. For example, LinkedIn lets you post a photo, while the AMWA Freelance Directory doesn't. But the AMWA Freelance Directory is easier to format than LinkedIn and lets you do more with font size. LinkedIn also has specific sections where you enter your information (e.g., summary, experience, publications, skills and endorsements, organizations, and education). In the Freelance Directory description you can include any information you'd like to, and you can create your own sections.

Test your LinkedIn and AMWA Freelance Directory profiles as soon as you've finalized them to make sure they read well and look right.

LinkedIn

A LinkedIn profile starts with your name and below that, a headline. Write a compelling headline based on your branding and your target audience. To the left of this is a space for a photo. Invest in a professional headshot, which you can also use on your website.

Include your contact information so people who view your profile can get in touch with you. Serdula says that people often forget to do this and then wonder why no one contacts them. Use the terrific free or low-cost resources that are available to craft your persuasive LinkedIn profile (see the resources at the end of this chapter).

Learn more about networking through LinkedIn in "Making a Name for Yourself: Networking and Reputation Building" (Chapter 7).

AMWA Freelance Directory

Most clients use the AMWA Freelance Directory to search for specific therapeutic areas (using the keywords search boxes). So be sure to include your areas of expertise. The search screen also allows clients to search by:

- Service and media types (by selecting categories)
- Last name
- City and state
- Degree
- Years of experience (0-5, 6-10, 11-15, 16-20, 21-25, 26+).

Since revising my AMWA Freelance Directory profile in 2014, after I heard LinkedIn guru Donna Serdula speak at the AMWA Delaware Valley Chapter freelance conference, my profile has been much more effective. Within a month, two potential clients contacted me with interesting opportunities. I was too busy to take the work on, but I was able to pass the opportunities on to colleagues. And I did speak to one of the potential clients about the possibility of working together in the future.

Develop Your Network and Website: An Introduction

Who you know—your network—is critical to marketing your freelance writing business. So is building your credibility as a freelance medical writer and a business owner, which requires a website. These last two essential marketing tools—your network and your website—are too important to cover briefly here.

Learn more about:

- "Making a Name for Yourself: Networking and Reputation Building" (Chapter 7).
- "Creating a Compelling Website" (Chapter 8).

Resources

ONLINE PRINTERS

Vistaprint (www.vistaprint.com): An economical and easy way to print business cards and other marketing materials. Upload your designs or use their templates. (Accessed May 9, 2014)

Staples: Staples.com:
Another economical and easy way to print business cards and other marketing materials. (Accessed May 9, 2014)

LINKEDIN

Free LinkedIn Makeover resources:
http://www.linkedin-makeover.com/linkedin-resources/
(Accessed May 9, 2014)

Donna Serdula, "The LinkedIn Makeover Book: Professional Secrets to a POWERFUL LinkedIn Profile," Second edition, 2013. www.linkedin-makeover.com/book

Chapter 7. Making a Name for Yourself: Networking and Reputation Building

"If people like you they'll listen to you, but if they trust you they'll do business with you.'
— Zig Ziglar

Growing your network and building your reputation go hand in hand. Who you know—a.k.a. your network—can be one of the most important factors in landing clients. But the people in your network need to trust you and know that you're competent and professional before they'll share opportunities or refer work to you.

Continually grow your network in person and through social media. Build your reputation by networking and participating in activities that highlight your trustworthiness, competence and reliability. Always:

- Give more than you take
- Be a useful resource to others
- Cultivate lasting and meaningful relationships with key people.

Essential Networking and Reputation-Building Tools

- Social networking through LinkedIn
- In-person networking through AMWA and other groups
- Volunteering for AMWA and other groups
- Publishing (e.g., AMWA Journal, e-zines, publications, and websites)
- Speaking and teaching (e.g., roundtables, presentations, and courses or workshops for AMWA or other groups)

Give More, Take Less

> **TIP:**
> Share knowledge, make introductions and mentor others.

Helping others without expecting anything in return—or giving more than you take—is the best way to build a solid network. Sharing relevant information and resources, and connecting people, boosts credibility and builds trust. The people you help will remember you when they have a freelance opportunity or something else to share. It's also easier to ask someone for help in the future if you've helped her or him in the past.

Helping Others

Through my active involvement in AMWA, I get a lot of emails from people asking for advice about medical writing or freelancing. Although I routinely work 50+ hours a week, usually at high speed and capacity, I always take a few minutes to respond. I answer the person's questions and offer tips and links to resources, ending with best wishes for success in medical writing. I don't do this because I expect that person to do something for me. Taking a few minutes to inspire a colleague, or offer resources that the person might not otherwise know about, makes me feel good. And I remember what it was like when I was trying to learn about medical writing.

Even though I don't expect anything in return, helping others has helped me. For example, I've gotten inquiries from people who said that someone in AMWA told them about me. Either they didn't remember the person's name or I didn't recognize it, but some action on my part led to the contact, which in some cases landed me a new client.

There's solid evidence behind the benefits of helping others. Adam Grant, a management professor at the University of Pennsylvania, found that people who give their time to others without expecting anything in return are more successful than people who don't do this. In 2013 (many years after I had started helping others), Grant published "Give and Take," a best-selling book about this.

Some Ways to Help Others

- Share information and resources:
  - Knowledge about the person's interests
  - Specific resources such as AMWA's Freelance Directory or Toolkit for New Medical Writers
  - Business books you've read
- Connect people:
  - Introduce people who do similar work
  - Introduce clients who need help to other freelance medical writers
- Mentor newer freelance medical writers (or medical writers who aren't freelancers)
- Refer work to other writers, but wisely:
  - Be sure you know the person you're referring to is competent and dependable

Annoying Others

Conversely, a blatant "Help me find clients" or "Hire me" is a real turnoff! People I meet for the first time have asked me to refer or subcontract work to them. I tell them the truth: that I only refer work to people I know well and have worked with in the past (this is almost always people I've worked with through volunteer activities for AMWA). But I always remember these people, and put them on my mental list of people to avoid.

Asking for information when you first meet someone is fine. And it's okay to mention the type of work you're looking for and ask whether the person you're talking to knows of organizations who hire freelance writers for this. But never blatantly ask someone you don't know well for a referral or a subcontract.

Focus on Key Contacts: Your Ecosystem

TIP:
Keep a spreadsheet of people you'd like to cultivate and your contacts with them. Review it regularly.

Networking, like all marketing, should be strategic. While you should be nice and helpful to everyone you meet (virtually or in person), focus most of your networking efforts on cultivating mutually beneficial relationships with key people. Freelance medical writers Jeanne McAdara-Berkowitz and Christine Welniak call this an ecosystem, defined by Dictionary.com as "a system of interconnecting and interacting parts."

You and the people in your ecosystem will share many things, including:

- Information
- Resources
- Advice
- Experiences, good and bad
- Solutions to problems
- Referrals to clients.

Sometimes you'll meet someone and immediately click. You just naturally start keeping in touch more. Or certain people could become more important to you over time. My ecosystem includes both types of people. But since I heard McAdara-Berkowitz and Welniak present on the ecosystem concept, I've been focused more on cultivating mutually beneficial relationships with key people.

Other freelance medical writers are a key part, but not all, of your ecosystem. Also cultivate mutually beneficial relationships with other people in medical writing. As you meet people, think about what you have in common and how you might help each other. If you think you might want the person to be part of your ecosystem, stay in touch and cultivate the relationship.

Ways to Stay in Touch

- Congratulate and compliment colleagues on professional achievements
- Comment on colleagues' work and activities (e.g., LinkedIn update, e-newsletter, blog post or new writing sample)
- Send links to relevant articles or resources
- Notify colleagues about events they may want to attend
- Share freelance opportunities you hear about
- Send cards (holiday, birthday, thank-you, etc.)
- Get together at the AMWA annual conference
- Meet for coffee or a meal in person, if you live close enough

Stay in touch with the people in your ecosystem at least two or three times a year. You can do this by email, phone, mail, in person or a combination of these methods. Focus on helping them. That way, you'll be comfortable asking for help when you need it.

Meet the Right People Face-to-Face

Many people, including me when I was starting out, are shy or afraid of networking. Think of networking as getting to know people, rather than selling your services, and it will be much easier.

Fortunately, the #1 networking source for freelance medical writers—AMWA—is made up of friendly, helpful people. Meet other medical writers, including freelancers like you, and people who work for organizations that are potential clients, by:

- Attending the AMWA annual conference
- Attending the annual AMWA-Delaware Valley Chapter freelance conference
- Attending events in your local chapter
- Participating in AMWA LinkedIn groups and AMWA community forums.

Strategic In-Person Networking

- Bring business cards (a lot) and your elevator pitch
- Set a realistic goal, like having good conversations with two people
- Listen for ways you can help the other person (e.g., by making introductions or sharing information and resources)
- Ask people questions about themselves
- Be pleasant and professional
- Don't spend too much time with one person

Follow up with the people you'd like to stay in touch with. An invitation to join your LinkedIn network or an email to say "nice to meet you" is an easy way to do this. Emailing the person with useful information or resources is even better (e.g., a link to an article related to work the person is doing or a resource on something you discussed). Include details of how and where you met.

TIP:
Make notes on the back of business cards to help you remember each person.

The Power of Volunteering

Cultivating relationships that are strong enough for people to trust you and know you're competent requires more than casual interaction. The best way to do this is to become an AMWA volunteer. Both the national organization and AMWA chapters have many interesting volunteer opportunities. Often, you'll meet—and have a chance to impress—AMWA leaders.

When I joined AMWA, I called the editor of the Delaware Valley Chapter's newsletter and offered to cover meetings. This provided useful content for the newsletter and enabled members who couldn't attend to learn what the meeting had covered. About 800 members of the chapter saw my byline on each article, and I began to build my reputation as a dependable volunteer among chapter leaders. I also volunteered to help at the registration desk before meetings, a quick easy task.

Over the years I've volunteered for AMWA in many ways. For the Delaware Valley chapter, I've been secretary and president, newsletter editor, freelance conference chair, presenter and roundtable leader, and more. For the national organization, I've been a delegate, a member of the AMWA Journal Freelance Forum panel, an annual conference committee member, presenter and roundtable leader, and more.

As I became more involved with AMWA, I began to get referrals—without asking for them. I also formed relationships with most of the people who became part of my ecosystem.

Connect with Others on LinkedIn and Other Social Networks

I've landed clients through LinkedIn and know other freelancers who've also done this. By building connections with colleagues and clients on LinkedIn, you can:

- Easily update colleagues and clients on your professional activities
- Keep track of them as they move around

- Gain access to the people your connections know.

> **TIP:**
> Use social networks strategically so you don't waste your time.

Some of my thoughts on LinkedIn follow, but I'm no expert. Donna Serdula is, so see her LinkedIn Makeover resources at the end of this chapter for how to really work LinkedIn.

Build Your LinkedIn Network

After writing a great profile (see Chapter 6), you need to start building your LinkedIn network by connecting with others. If you want people to find you, you need to be part of their networks.

Your LinkedIn Network

A LinkedIn network is made up of:

- **First-degree connections:** People who invite you to be part of their network or accept your invitation to be part of your network.

- **Second-degree connections:** People connected to your first-degree connections, whom you can invite to connect with you.

- **Third-degree connections:** People connected to your second-degree connections. You can connect with them, but you may need to ask your second-degree connection for an introduction (depending on how the person has set up his or her account).

- **Members of your LinkedIn groups**: You can contact fellow group members by sending a message on LinkedIn or participating in discussions.

Who Should You Connect With?

I only connect with people I know. My connections are a reflection on me, and I don't want to introduce someone I don't know well to another connection. If I get an invitation to connect from someone I don't know, I politely explain this. LinkedIn also recommends only making first-degree connections with people you know and trust.

Some people, including Serdula, believe it's better to connect with almost anyone to build your network and appear more often in search results. But if too many people respond to your invitations to connect with "I don't know" or "Report as spam," LinkedIn will restrict or terminate your account.

Other people connect with people they don't know if they're part of the same industry. If you get an invitation from someone you don't know who might be a good connection, check out his/her profile before deciding whether to accept the invitation. If you decide to accept, ask how you can help each other.

Making the Connection

When you invite people to join your network, write a personal message. It's very annoying when I get a standard "I'd like to add you to my professional network on LinkedIn" invitation. We're writers, so take a few seconds to write something interesting, or at least personal (e.g., about how you know each other.)

Getting Noticed

Having lots of connections won't do you much good unless you use LinkedIn actively and attract positive attention. LinkedIn has two useful features for freelancers: updates and groups.

Providing Interesting Information through Updates

Updates are short notes (600 characters maximum) that keep your connections thinking about you through the periodic network updates LinkedIn sends out. The top of your LinkedIn home page, next to your photo, has a "Share an update" bar where you enter the update. You can share:

- Expert advice
- Links to interesting news
- Links to interesting articles
- Upcoming events
- Questions and requests
- Examples of your work, if relevant and interesting to your connections
- More.

You can include Web links and attach files to updates. Your home page also has updates from people in your network. Read these, and the periodic network updates LinkedIn sends out, to get good ideas for your updates and see what to avoid.

Sample Updates

Update #1

Lori De Milto *(LinkedIn automatically adds your name above the update)*

"Survey finds many medical tests and procedures are unnecessary, even harmful: http://lnkd.in/ddV55Rg"

(LinkedIn automatically added this blurb below my update)

Survey: Physicians are Aware that Many Medical Tests and Procedures...

Survey looks at physician attitudes on overuse of medical services in the U.S., and shows that more than half of physicians think they are in the best position to address the problem and are responsible for making sure patients avoid...

Update #2
Lori De Milto
"is leading a roundtable on marketing at the 2014 AMWA freelance conference" (with a link to the conference brochure)

Update #3
Lori De Milto
"Statin users eating more calories and fat than in past, study in JAMA Internal Medicine says" (with a link to the study)
(LinkedIn automatically added this blurb below my update)
Gluttony in the Time of Statins?
Both dietary modification and use of statins can lower blood cholesterol. The increase in caloric intake among the general population is reported to have plateaued in the last decade, but no study has...

Highlighting Expertise and Building Relationships through Groups

People who participate in groups get four times the number of profile views as people who don't, according to LinkedIn. Groups let you share your expertise and build relationships. Good groups for freelance medical writers include AMWA, Medical Marketing & Communications Group, Drug Information Association, the Freelance Writers Connection and alumni groups. Ways to find other groups include:

- Checking out the groups potential clients belong to (see Groups near the bottom of their profiles)
- Checking out the groups other freelance medical writers belong to (see Groups near the bottom of their profiles)
- Taking suggestions from LinkedIn
- Doing a general search for groups (under the Interests tab at the top).

Participating in Group Discussions

When you comment or start a discussion, your name and the headline from your LinkedIn profile appear above the comment or just below the headline of your discussion topic. This is a great mini ad for your business.

Sample Comment Header

Lori De Milto
Professional Medical Writer ● Delivers Targeted Copy and Content ● On Time, Every Time.

After you join a group, start participating in discussions. This is a great way to highlight your expertise and start building relationships, especially if you're providing a solution to a problem. In fact, a colleague of mine landed a client by offering suggestions in a discussion.

> **TIP:**
> Get ideas for starting discussions from other discussions in your groups.

Once you've gotten the feel of a group, start discussions yourself. Focus on topics of relevance and interest to group members. Examples of discussion topics in the AMWA group include:

- Advice and discussion on how to enhance the quality of posters
- A question about guidelines for retaining business records and related documents
- Best practices in CME grant writing, with a link to an article on this.

Other Social Networks

Explore other social networks, including AMWA community forums, which might be useful to you. But be strategic about social networking and limit the amount of time you spend on this. It's very easy to spend a lot of time on social networking without getting enough return to justify the investment.

AMWA Community Forums

AMWA community forums, in the Members Only section of AMWA's website, let you connect with peers in various areas, including:

- Essentials of writing, such as tools and resources (discussion about tools, tips and tricks for medical writing)
- Professional communities, such as freelancing, regulatory writing, medical device writing, CME, and writing for lay audiences.

Twitter and Others

I tried Twitter for a few years, but didn't think it helped me market my services. Some freelance medical writers help clients manage their social networks (e.g., tweeting or blogging for them). If you do, or want to do, this type of work, then you need to use social networks more intensely for your business.

Build Your Reputation

In B2B marketing (marketing from one business to another), your company image, brand and reputation are crucial.

Being Responsive, Professional and Polite

Virtually everything you do affects your image, brand and reputation. Be responsive, professional and polite to everyone. You never know when a contact will turn into a client—or refer you to a client. I've met potential clients in some unusual places:

- On safari in Tanzania
- At the home of a friend who is not a medical writer
- In a plane heading to Israel.

Your child's teacher or the person in front of you in the supermarket could be a great resource for you. But if you make a bad first impression, that person will forget meeting you, or worse, vow to have nothing to do with you.

Marketing is all about planting seeds. You never know where one will grow.

Showing and Sharing your Expertise

Publishing, speaking and teaching are also great ways to share your expertise and build your reputation.

Publishing, Speaking and Teaching for AMWA

AMWA offers you a convenient way to publish, speak and teach. You could write a feature article for the AMWA Journal or a shorter, less formal article for a section like Practical Matters or covering a session at the annual conference. If your chapter has a newsletter, volunteer to write for that. If your chapter doesn't have a newsletter, volunteer to start one!

The annual conference needs many roundtable discussion leaders, presenters and teachers. Each year, AMWA puts out a call for proposals for roundtable discussions, posters and open sessions. Leading a roundtable is a fun and easy way to dip a toe in teaching.

Other Opportunities

You can also write and submit articles to:

- E-zines (electronic online magazines)
- Community newspapers
- Trade journals
- Other publications

- Websites and online article directories (which collect articles that editors and publishers can use for free)
- Newsletters or publications of other organizations or associations you belong to.

Find speaking and teaching opportunities through other associations and organizations, adult learning centers and colleges.

Resources

BOOKS

Adam Grant, "Give and Take," 2013. http://www.giveandtake.com/Home/Book, Named one of the best books of 2013 by Amazon, Apple, the Financial Times, and the Wall Street Journal; one of Oprah's riveting reads, Fortune's must-read business books, Harvard Business Review's ideas that shaped management, and the *Washington Post's* books every leader should read.

Donna Serdula, "The LinkedIn Makeover Book: Professional Secrets to a POWERFUL LinkedIn Profile" Second edition, 2013. linkedin-makeover.com/book

C.J. Hayden, "Get Clients Now! A 28-Day Marketing Program for Professionals, Consultants, and Coaches," 2013. http://www.amazon.com/Get-Clients-Now-Professionals-Consultants

Susan RoAne, "How to Work a Room, Revised edition: Your Essential Guide to Savvy Socializing," 2007. http://www.amazon.com/How-Work-Room-Revised-Edition/dp/0061238678

Juli Monroe. "The Enthusiastic Networker," 2011.
http://www.amazon.com/The-Enthusiastic-Networker-Juli-
Monroe/dp/1883953405

ARTICLES

Free LinkedIn Makeover resources: linkedin-
makeover.com/linkedin-resources/(Accessed 4/26/14)

LinkedIn for small business:
smallbusiness.linkedin.com/personal-branding.html (Accessed
4/26/14)

"Sharing Ideas, Questions, Articles, and Website Links":
help.linkedin.com/app/answers/detail/a_id/434/kw/updates
(Accessed 4/26/14)

"Starting a Discussion in Groups":
help.linkedin.com/app/answers/detail/a_id/1622/ft/eng
(Accessed 4/26/14)

ASSOCIATION

AMWA

Information on contributing to the AMWA Journal:
amwa.org/volunteer_amwajournal and
amwa.org/files/Publications/Journal_instructions_2013.p
df (Accessed 4/26/14)

Annual Conference Call for Proposals, with information on
how to lead a roundtable:
http://www.amwa.org/2014_call_for_proposals
(Accessed 4/26/14)

Volunteer Opportunities:
amwa.org/content.asp?contentid=72 (Accessed 4/26/14)

Chapter 8. Creating a Compelling Website

"Marketing is a contest for people's attention."
— Seth Godin

If you want to be taken seriously, you need a website. It's a key part of marketing any business today. But this essential marketing tool for freelance medical writers takes time, effort and money to develop. So it's okay to make developing your website part of your phase 2 marketing.

Put the Web to Work for You

- Advertise your writing skills
- Show what you can do for clients
- Brand your services
- Build more credibility as a writer
- Establish yourself as a business owner

Content that's well written and a professional design that's easy to navigate are the main components of a compelling website for a freelance medical writer. While you'll need to pay for a Web designer, it's well worth the expense. Once you've done that and launched your website, it will be a low-cost marketing tool.

Understand Essential Web Content

A compelling website for a freelance medical writer isn't complex or lengthy. If you've developed your LinkedIn and AMWA Freelance Directory profiles, you'll have much of the information you need for your content.

Before starting to write your content, visit the websites of other freelance medical writers. AMWA's Freelance Directory makes it easy to do this. When I revised my website in 2008, I went through the listings and visited the website of every writer who had one. Make notes about things you like and don't like, including Web page sections and the language used.

Also, look at the websites of larger companies in marketing, medical communications, advertising and so forth for inspiration. You can find some of these by looking at the organizations AMWA members work for and checking out relevant websites, or through Web searches.

Anatomy of a Freelance Medical Writer's Website

- Home page
- About you
- Services
- Portfolio (or Writing Samples)
- Clients
- Testimonials (which can be combined with clients)
- Contact

If you're just starting out, you won't have pages for clients and testimonials. That's okay.

Home Page

> **TIP:**
> Write the rest of your content first and then come back to your home page.

Make a strong first impression online with your home page. A compelling home page:
- Visually conveys your brand (name, tagline and logo)

- Sets the tone and personality of your website
- Has a short, clear description of your services
- Entices a viewer to learn more.

Although your home page should be short, what you say here is crucial. Do plenty of research (visiting websites of other freelance medical writers) and use your research about your target market and your branding (covered in Chapters 3 and 4).

About You

You can call this "About," "About [your first and last name]," "About [first name]," or even "About Me," like I did. My website has a very bold informal tone so "About Me" works well. Most medical writers probably want to be a little more conservative.

Having a photo of yourself on your website helps clients see that you and your services are real. Most freelance medical writers with good websites I've seen put the photo on the "About" page. Use a professional headshot.

Start the "About" page with some brief sales content—why the viewer should use your services. Some freelance medical writers use this page for a brief summary of their experience and accomplishments. Others, like me, include details on education, experience, awards and honors, and other professional accomplishments. But this is not a resume. Some of the information is the same, but you'll present it in a more interesting way and with less detail.

Some freelance medical writers include a link to their resume or a bio. You can also include a link to your LinkedIn profile. I've also seen links to the pages on services, portfolio and testimonials in this section.

Services

Simple bulleted lists work great here. The categories you use depend on the type of work you do. Sample categories include:

- Services (e.g., writing, editing, consulting, publication management and training)
- Media (e.g., journal articles, continuing medical education, white papers, newsletters, Web content, blogs and social media)
- Areas of expertise, topic areas or therapeutic areas (e.g., cardiovascular disease, diabetes and oncology).

Some freelance medical writers start this section with some brief sales content. That's fine.

Portfolio or Writing Samples

Samples of your work are a great sales tool and something clients expect to see. If your work is proprietary and you can't post or link to writing samples, there are other ways for you to highlight your writing skills (including your website content) and the work that you've done.

Use categories to make it easy for potential clients to find what they're most interested in—and to highlight the type of work you really want to do. The exact categories depend on the type of work you do. I categorize my samples by the audiences I write for:

- Consumers and patients
- Physicians and healthcare professionals
- Policymakers, academia and other audiences

I put "consumers and patients" first because this is the type of writing I like best.

Other freelance medical writers use types of projects as categories (e.g., selected proprietary work, feature writing and Web content).

TIP:
Print out quality copies of website content you've written. If the client later changes what you wrote, post a scan of the printout as a sample.

Showcasing Proprietary Work

If your work is proprietary, there are several ways to share your writing and your work:

- Your website content
- A list of projects you've worked on
- Project descriptions
- Unpaid samples.

Your website content is a great sample of your writing skills. A list of projects (e.g., a white paper and slide deck on an insulin pump or fact sheets on new oncology drugs) will at least tell potential clients the type of work you've done.

If you don't have any or enough samples from paid work that you can post or link to, develop a few unpaid samples. Do this by volunteering to write articles for your AMWA chapter's newsletter, submitting a story idea to the AMWA Journal, writing for other groups you belong to, writing a few articles for syndication, etc.

If you want to work in a new area, consider developing a "spec" sample: something that shows you can do what you want to do. For example, if you want to work in CME, write part of a CME program for a disease.

Project Descriptions

TIP:
Use project descriptions to add impact to writing samples and highlight your skills.

Using project descriptions along with writing samples is an idea I picked up from a presentation at an AMWA annual conference. You can post project descriptions even if your work is proprietary and you can't post samples, but you'll have to leave out some details.

Project descriptions let you highlight what you did on each project, including any skills beyond medical writing. For example,

I've started several newsletters for clients, which is very different than just writing assigned stories for a newsletter. I enjoyed that and would be glad to do similar work for other clients.

You can also highlight the organizations you've worked for (e.g., xyz hospital, one of the top hospitals in the Northeast) in your project descriptions. Working for prestigious clients boosts your credibility.

Anatomy of a Project Description

Client*:
- Name
- Brief description from the organization's website
- Location

Project, such as:
- Journal article
- Newsletter
- Web content

Audience, such as:
- Physicians
- Consumers
- Patients

Role (where you can highlight skills other than writing), such as:
- Conducted research, interviewed physicians and patients and wrote the article
- Developed the content outline for the website and wrote all content
- Managed the project from concept through design and printing.

* If your work is proprietary, leave out the client's name and location and just describe the type of client (e.g., a pharmaceutical company).

Clients

> **TIP:**
> Include a testimonial from a satisfied client on this Web page.

The "Clients" page is also easy to develop. Choose categories that let you highlight your most important services. Most writers do this by type of work (e.g., CME, monographs, newsletters and website content). I did mine by the type of clients I work with (e.g., hospitals, foundations, associations and agencies). Since I love working with hospitals, I put them first.

For each client, I include a brief description. Saying that I'm working with "one of the nation's leading academic medical centers" or "the nation's largest health and healthcare philanthropic organization" is more impressive than simply listing organization names.

Testimonials

What others say about you is far more powerful than what you say about yourself. Testimonials from satisfied clients let you:

- Market your business
- Strengthen your brand
- Build your credibility
- Enhance your reputation.

You can combine the testimonials page with the clients page.

Asking for Testimonials

You can ask any client who is happy with your work for a testimonial, but it's best to ask clients you've worked with for a while, in my opinion. Explain how you'll use the testimonial, and that you will send it the person for final approval before posting. If you already have some testimonials, send along an example.

In my experience, most clients are happy to provide testimonials. If someone doesn't want to provide a testimonial, politely thank the person for considering it and move on.

Getting Approval for Testimonials

When someone agrees to write a testimonial and sends it to you, do any editing necessary to correct mistakes or to shorten a very long testimonial. Then add the identifying information you plan to use below the testimonial (e.g., client's name and organization, perhaps the location). Email this to the client asking for final approval. Also ask whether the client needs to get approval from the organization; some larger organizations may require this.

Never use anything that someone has said about you without asking for permission first. If, for example, a client writes in an email that you did a terrific job on a project, ask if you can use that in a testimonial. But do not just use it without getting the client's approval.

Contact

Make it easy for people to contact you with a simple contact page. Include your name, email address, phone number, and address (at least your city and state).

Don't use a form template. Your goal is to build relationships with prospective clients, and contact forms are distant and annoying. The last thing you want to do after developing a compelling website that's motivated a prospective client to contact you is to annoy that person.

Entice Potential Clients with Compelling Content

Writing Web content is very different than writing for print. Web users scan, reading only 20 to 28 percent of the average Web page, according to Web usability expert Jakob Nielsen. They stay on an average page less than a minute, and many stay 10 seconds or less. If Web users don't find what they want fast, they leave the website.

Draw users into your website and keep them there long enough to do what you want them to do through compelling Web content. Use what you learned from your market research and your branding to develop messages that will entice potential clients and motivate them to spend more time on your website.

Essential Features of Compelling Web Content

Tone:
- Informal
- Concise

Writing:
- Short paragraphs
- Simple sentences
- Simple, familiar words
- Active voice
- Lots of verbs

Messages:
- Benefits-focused
- Most important information first

Emphasis on key messages:
- Attention-grabbing headlines
- Lots of enticing subheads
- Bulleted and numbered lists

Be Conversational and Concise

Compelling content is informal and concise. Write like you're having a conversation with a friend to make your content more personal and inviting.

Focus on the benefits you offer clients. Use attention-grabbing headlines and subheads to convey key messages fast. Put the most important information first.

Chunk Content

Break up (or chunk) information into topics and sub-topics. Use headings and subheads to:

- Draw users in
- Help users quickly find information
- Make scanning easier.

Engage Users

Keep paragraphs short and sentences simple. On the Web, a one-sentence paragraph is fine. Use simple, familiar words that your target audience understands. Avoid jargon, and avoid or limit confusing acronyms and abbreviations. Use the active voice and lots of verbs. This makes content easier to understand and more powerful.

Emphasize Key Points

Lists create a sense of immediacy and emphasize key points:

- Numbered lists work great for instructions and steps.
- Bulleted lists convey non-sequential information (e.g., options to choose from).

Show Off Compelling Content with a Captivating Design

Hire a Web designer to make your compelling content look professional and captivating. Ask for a content management system so you can easily update the content yourself. Technology definitely isn't my forte, but using my content management system is easy. If I can do it, you can too.

To find a good Web designer, ask freelance medical writers whose websites you like about their Web designers. Check out the websites of these designers to see what else they've done.

Your Web designer can help you with all of the technical stuff too, like how to get a domain name (your URL) that's the same as or very close to your company name. Pay for a Web hosting service. There are free services, but you won't look like a professional if you use one.

SEO and Freelance Medical Writers

SEO (search engine optimization) involves writing Web content that search-engine algorithms will find and rank highly in search results. The goal is to increase the number of visitors to a website.

While SEO is often lauded as crucial to the success of a website, it's extremely unlikely that potential clients will be doing general searches for freelance medical writers. If they do, they'd get so many results that they'd never wade through them.

As freelance medical writers, we need to drive traffic to our websites through our other marketing. In my view, there's no reason to spend any time, effort or money on SEO. There's just too little (probably no) return on investment for us.

And it's not a one-time process. The rules of SEO change constantly and you'd be spending a lot of time, money or both for little or no gain.

Use Your Website to Market Your Business

TIP:
Send out a postcard to announce the launch of your website.

Once your website is live, you need to market it. When I revamped my website in 2008, I created a postcard announcing the launch of my new website and sent it to colleagues, clients and selected potential clients. While I didn't land any new clients from this, I did form a mutually beneficial relationship with a colleague who liked the postcard and was also an active marketer.

These days, you could also announce your website launch through a LinkedIn update. That's a good idea, but I'd also recommend doing a direct mail postcard. This will make more of an impression than one of many LinkedIn updates your connections see every week.

Include your URL on all marketing materials, including your email signature and business cards. Cross-market your website on your LinkedIn and Freelance Directory profiles. This is very effective because if people are reading your profiles, they're just one click away from your website.

Keep Content Current

Web content isn't static. As a freelance medical writer, you don't need to constantly update your website. But you should review it at least quarterly. Add new writing samples or project descriptions. Update anything that's not current.

Every January, change the year of the website and make all other necessary quantitative updates (e.g., years in business).

Resources

BOOKS

Janice (Ginny) Redish, "Letting Go of the Words: Writing Web Content that Works," Second edition. San Francisco, CA: Morgan Kauffmann Publishers, 2012. www.amazon.com/Letting-Words-Second-Edition-Technologies/dp/0123859301

Shama Hyder Kabani, "The Zen of Social Media Marketing, An Easier Way to Build Credibility, Generate Buzz, and Increase

Revenue," 2012. http://www.amazon.com/The-Zen-Social-Media-Marketing/dp/1937856151

ARTICLE

Barry Feldman, "Writing Content: 21 Tips for Getting it Right," http://socialmediatoday.com/feldmancreative/1611616/right-way-write-content (Accessed 4/3/14)

WEBSITES

Nielsen Norman Group. A variety of articles on Web usability and related topics. www.nngroup.com/articles. (Accessed 5/12/14)

Chapter 9. Making Marketing Work for You (Part 2): Effective Marketing Tools

"You can't wait for inspiration.
You have to go after it with a club."
— Jack London

Add effective marketing tools after you've developed your essential marketing tools (Chapter 6). The more you market, the more business you'll land. Consider your budget, preferences and marketing goal when choosing from the marketing tools that work for freelance medical writers.

Effective Marketing Tools

Cards and gifts:
- Holiday cards and gifts for clients
- Special occasion cards and gifts for clients
- Holiday cards for prospects and colleagues

Direct mail:
- Self-mailer
- Postcard
- Letter

Email marketing:
- E-newsletter

Printed marketing materials:
- Thank-you and note cards
- Postcards

Stay in Touch with Cards and Gifts

This is so simple and effective! At the holidays, send cards to your clients, prospects (whom you've had contact with) and colleagues. It's a quick, easy way to stay in touch. I buy my cards from UNICEF's business collection, so I'm also supporting a good cause. My cards are in the mail the day after Thanksgiving, so people get them before they're inundated with cards.

TIP:
Buy high-quality business holiday cards. Send them early.

Send your regular clients a gift at the holidays, along with a card. Since I live just outside of Philadelphia, I send my clients gift trays of luscious homemade chocolate-covered pretzels from Anthony's Chocolate House in Philadelphia's famous Italian Market. They look forward to getting these each year.

You can also send smaller gifts. When I was doing communications for a university in my pre-freelance life, a printer I worked with always stopped by at the holidays with a tin of Danish cookies. This didn't cost much, but getting the gift made me smile. It also made this printer stand out in my mind as a preferred vendor (among printers who did high-quality work). And of course, I enjoyed the cookies.

When you know about a special occasion in a client's professional or personal life (e.g., a promotion, wedding or birth of a baby), definitely send a card. Consider sending a gift too, like a nice photo frame for a wedding or the birth of a baby.

Target Prospects with Direct Mail and Email Marketing

Direct mail and email marketing let you target your best prospects and go directly to them with a relevant offer. Researching organizations and developing your mailing list takes a lot of time and effort, but it's worth it.

You can find ideas and inspiration anywhere. For example, the realtor who sold us our house 23 years ago sends us a few postcards every year with seasonal recipes or gardening tips on one side and some marketing copy and her contact information on the other. If we decide to sell our house, or know someone who wants to buy or sell a house, we'll think of her because of those postcards.

Landing Great Clients Through Direct Mail

Direct mail, and now email marketing, is one of my most effective marketing tools. Back in 1997 when I was starting out, I used direct mail extensively. In my first year or so, I sent three flyers to about 250 people each, spending about $7,000. It was worth every penny. Within 18 months, I had as much business as I wanted. And I'm still working with two of the clients I landed through that first direct mail campaign.

Developing my mailing lists back then was much more work than it is now, since the Web was in its infancy. I searched the AMWA Member Directory for companies I might want to work for and contacts in those companies. To develop the rest of my mailing list, I went to the library and searched directories of hospitals, healthcare associations and other healthcare organizations for other potential clients. All of this took many hours.

Since then, whenever I've wanted to land new clients, or explore or work more in specific medical writing markets, I've done another direct mail campaign. These campaigns were smaller and more targeted. For example, I did separate campaigns for hospitals, National Cancer Institute cancer centers and hospitals with integrative medicine programs. Other freelance medical writers I know who've tried direct mail after hearing about my success have also landed clients.

Follow these four easy steps for direct mail and email marketing that works:

1. Develop targeted lists for direct mail and email marketing.

2. Write compelling direct mail and email marketing copy.
3. Design captivating direct mail and email marketing pieces.
4. Plan your campaign.

Although the steps are easy, they do take time, especially developing your lists.

Developing Targeted Lists

Develop lists of organizations you'd like to work for (organization, appropriate contact person or people, email address and mailing address) for your direct mail and email marketing. This is a lot of work, but it's well worth it.

People will give your direct mail pieces to colleagues or forward your marketing emails to them, so you don't even necessarily have to have the right person on your mailing list. Two of my clients (including one I've been working with since 1998) were not the people on my mailing lists, but colleagues who knew they needed freelance help passed my direct mail pieces on to them.

Use your market research and your marketing plan (the type of clients and specific clients you've identified) as the starting place for your lists. Identify more prospects through:

- The AMWA Member Directory
- Your LinkedIn network
- AMWA Jobs Online (which includes freelance opportunities)
- Online directories and leading company lists (e.g., Medical Marketing & Media top 100 agencies, Insight Company Monitor top 50 pharma companies or American Hospital Association directory).

Look for names of senior people (e.g., managers, directors, associate directors or vice presidents) in the departments that you'd like to work for, like medical writing, medical communications, communications or marketing.

As you're developing mailing lists, categorize them by priority (e.g., priority #1, priority #2 and priority #3), your special interests or both. For example, I have separate mailing lists for hospitals, National Cancer Institute cancer centers, integrative medicine centers and general prospects. Also develop lists of clients and colleagues, who may know of other opportunities.

> **TIP:**
> Include organizations looking for full-time medical writers on your mailing lists. They may also use freelancers.

Writing Direct Mail and Email Marketing

In these days where so much of professional life revolves around the Web, social media and email, a well written, professionally designed and printed direct mail piece stands out. While some types of email marketing, like a quarterly e-newsletter, can be effective for freelance medical writers, I'd be very cautious about sending people unsolicited emails. We all get way too many emails every day, and the last thing you want to do is annoy prospective clients.

Most of the principles of writing direct mail also apply to email marketing. The main difference is that you don't have things like mailing panels and envelopes in email marketing. And the design of email marketing is generally simpler.

Your direct mail pieces can be self mailers (also called flyers), letters or postcards. Self-mailers, which highlight creativity and your brand, require really strong marketing messages and great design. They are typically 8.5" x 11" with copy on both sides, and are mailed without an envelope.

Letters let you apply direct mail principles in a more subdued way than self-mailers, but you'll need to address each one to a person. Keep it to one page. Postcards are best for short, specific messages, like announcing the launch of a new website.

Whatever type of direct mail you choose, the writing must be clever and easy to read, and get to the point fast. Like Web content, people will scan your direct mail piece rather than read it word for word.

Writing Direct Mail Copy that Sells

- Give the most important information first, focusing on the benefits you offer clients.
- Convey key messages fast with attention-grabbing headlines and subheads.
- Keep paragraphs short and sentences simple.
- Be informal, like you're having a conversation with a friend.
- Use bulleted lists to create a sense of immediacy and emphasize key points.
- Use the active voice and active verbs to create a sense of urgency.
- Include a call to action (e.g., Call me at xxx-xxx-xxxx to discuss your project today).

A direct mail self-mailer has three outside and three inside sections. The outside sections are:

- Mailing section: Mailing addresses (yours and the prospect's) and a sentence or phrase to draw people into the self-mailer
- Middle section: Another marketing message
- Bottom section: Copy that ties into the inside headline (see below). When a potential client opens the self-mailer, the bottom section is visible just below the headline before the mailer is unfolded completely

The inside sections are:

- Top section: Headline and graphic
- Middle and bottom sections: Marketing messages, call to action, logo and your contact information

---

Example: My Self-Mailer for Integrative Medicine Centers

Outside mailing section:

Attract more people to your integrative medicine center

Main headline on inside top section:

Attract more minds, bodies and spirits

Outside bottom section:

With targeted copy and content by Lori De Milto Writer for Rent LLC

(followed by brief, bulleted professional highlights)

The inside middle section has copy about helping people optimize health and healing and how targeted copy and content can help integrative medicine centers attract more patients. After this, on the inside bottom section, is the call to action and my logo and contact information. The outside third section says:

Help more people optimize health and healing

If you're writing a letter, always include a P.S. It's one of the most read parts of a direct mail letter. Write something that will make the person go back and read the entire letter, if he or she hasn't already done that.

| TIP: |
| Maximize the impact of direct mail letters with a P.S. |

Freelance medical writers shouldn't use some principles of direct mail, in my opinion. Traditionally, direct mail includes an offer (e.g., a free product or a discount on the first order) and a deadline for responding to the offer. If you can think of a free product to give your prospects that will impress them and highlight your experience, by all means go ahead and make the offer. Giving a discount on the first "order" though, is a terrible idea. I've never included a free product or discount, and my direct mail campaigns have been very successful.

Likewise, imposing a deadline may work when selling widgets, but it's a bad idea for freelance medical writers. Clients will contact us when they need us, not when we tell them to contact us. A deadline will only annoy your prospects.

Email Marketing

A quarterly e-newsletter is a great way to stay in touch with clients, prospective clients (with whom you've had contact) and colleagues while sharing useful information. It also highlights your writing skills. Focus on the needs of your target audience, but do it in a way that highlights your expertise.

One issue of my e-newsletter, for example, had a feature story on getting your message across on the Web, since I love writing Web content. I tied another story into that by providing statistics on the use of the Web for health information, with links to the studies. The statistics and the links to more information gave my clients and prospects useful information.

The next story offered tips on being more successful by helping others and a link to a best-selling book on the subject. This was also relevant and useful to clients and prospects, as well as to my colleagues.

Only after sharing all of this useful information did I briefly promote myself, through descriptions of and links to some of my recent projects, followed by my then upcoming participation in the 2014 AMWA-DVC freelance conference.

Writing an Impressive E-Newsletter

- Develop a name and benefits-oriented tagline.
- Write a subject line that will entice people to read.
- Be concise:
  - Short articles and paragraphs
  - Simple sentences

- Convey key messages fast:
  - o Attention-grabbing headlines and subheads
  - o Active voice and active verbs
  - o Bulleted lists
- Be informal (Write like you're talking to a friend.)
- Develop a standard format:
  - o Feature story
  - o Regular columns with useful information, like tips and resources, relevant news or statistics, and recommended reading
  - o Regular promotional columns, like recent projects, upcoming professional events, and other news
- Call to action (if desired):
  - o A short blurb about your services with contact information
- Editorial box (at the end):
  - o Copyright information, basic newsletter description and contact information
- Information on unsubscribing

Designing Direct Mail and Email Marketing

This is another job for a professional graphic designer. If you want results, your direct mail and email marketing must look professional. Use your logo and other elements of your branding (colors, fonts, etc.) so that all of your marketing (print and online) has a family look.

TIP:
Print direct mail pieces quickly and easily through Vistaprint.com.

Designing Direct Mail

If you plan to do a lot of direct mail and other printed marketing pieces and you have an interest in and aptitude for graphic design, consider investing in desktop publishing software (e.g., Adobe InDesign). Then you can ask your designer to develop the first direct mail piece for you and give you a file you can use as a template for future direct mail pieces. Your designer can also provide files for other marketing pieces that you can update yourself.

Don't do this unless you have some basic graphic design skills. I do, so I bought InDesign and had my designer give me files for my logo and a template that I use in my direct mail pieces.

Designing Email Marketing

With Web-based services like Constant Contact and Mail Chimp, it's easy to design a professional e-newsletter using one of their templates. But again, unless you've got a really good sense of graphic design, have your designer develop a sample issue for you. This will then become your template for future issues.

TIP:
Choose a template that's optimized for mobile users, since many people read their email on smartphones or tablets.

Use large fonts that are easy to read, including on smartphones and tables. Experts suggest a font size of at least 11 points for text and 22 points for headlines. Subhead font size should be about 14 or 16 points. Use colors that contrast so the email is easy for people to read.

Before sending out an e-newsletter, or any email marketing, send a test email to yourself. See how it looks on a mobile device (smartphone or tablet), a PC and a Mac. And, of course, make sure there are no mistakes.

Planning Your Direct Mail and Email Campaign

Prospective clients need to be thinking of you when they need a freelance writer. This means you have to reach them with your message enough times (marketing frequency) that they'll remember you, but not so often that you annoy them. Some marketing experts say you need to reach a prospect three to five times to make a sale; others say seven is the magic number.

During my first direct mail campaign (three self-mailers, each to about 250 people over 18 months), some prospective clients contacted me within days of receiving the first flyer. Others hired me after receiving the second or third flyer. So I learned firsthand about the importance of frequency.

Making an Impact with Frequent, Well-Crafted Direct Mail and Email

A combined direct mail and email campaign with three to seven messages a year seems about right to me. Direct mail will have more impact on your prospects—and be more likely to be read by them—than email. Everyone is overwhelmed with email these days. A well-crafted direct mail piece, on the other hand, will stand out and make a good impression.

Also, you can send direct mail to all prospects. But don't send email to anyone you haven't had contact with.

Sample Direct Mail and Email Campaign

First quarter:
- Direct mail self-mailer or letter
- Email newsletter

Second quarter:
- Direct mail postcard
- Email newsletter

Third quarter:
- Direct mail self-mailer or letter
- Email newsletter

Fourth quarter:
- Email newsletter

Enhance Your Image with Printed Marketing Materials

Develop printed marketing materials with your brand to give or send to people: thank-you cards, note cards, postcards, and other relevant marketing materials, like bookmarks. Sending people thank-you cards and notes is an easy way to enhance your image. You can do this by email, but the impact will be far less. I've always sent people thank-you cards when they've done something nice for me, but I just used regular thank-you cards. After a speaker at the 2013 AMWA-DVC freelance conference suggested using personalized business thank-you cards, I ordered these. She also suggested sending small flat note cards to people if a thank-you card wasn't quite right. I ordered these too. Both have my name, business name, tagline, logo and contact information.

Some freelance medical writers have postcards that describe their services. After I saw a stack of these on display at an AMWA annual conference, I decided to develop a postcard for my business. I know another writer who uses a postcard for both direct mail and displays.

When I meet people, I also hand out bookmarks with a quote on one side and my business name, tagline, logo and contact information on the other. The idea came from a visit to a library bookstore in Florida, which gave out bookmarks with purchases. One side had a quote about reading and the other had information about the library bookstore.

Resources

ONLINE PRINTERS

Vistaprint: vistaprint.com
Quick, easy, economical printing for flyers, postcards and more. Upload your designs or use their templates.

Staples.com: Another economical and easy way to print business cards and other marketing materials.

LINKEDIN

Free LinkedIn Makeover resources: http://www.linkedin-makeover.com/linkedin-resources/

LinkedIn for small business: smallbusiness.linkedin.com/personal-branding.html

Donna Serdula, "The LinkedIn Makeover Book: Professional Secrets to a POWERFUL LinkedIn Profile," Second edition, 2013. www.linkedin-makeover.com/book

DIRECT MAIL

Craig Simpson with Dan S. Kennedy. "The Direct Mail Solution: A Business Owner's Guide to Building a Lead-Generating, Sales-Driving, Money-Making Direct-Mail Campaign. Entrepreneur Media," 2014. http://www.amazon.com/Direct-Mail-Solution-Lead-Generating-Sales-Driving/dp/1599185180

Claire Sutton, 10 Writing Tips for your Direct Marketing Campaign, www.agencypost.com/10-writing-tips-for-your-direct-marketing-campaign/ (Accessed April 17, 2014)

ZAPCO
www.zapcopaper.com
High quality paper for self-mailers, postcards and note cards (for use on small runs of direct mail pieces in your printer).

EMAIL MARKETING SERVICE PROVIDER

Constant Contact: constantcontact.com
"Suite of tools helps you reach, engage, and acquire new customers through email, events, and social media"

MailChimp: mailchimp.com
"Online email marketing solution to manage contacts, send emails and track results"

EMAIL MARKETING

Sarah Chapple, "The Dos and Don'ts of Successful Small Business Email Marketing."
http://smallbusinessesdoitbetter.com/2014/03/the-dos-and-donts-of-successful-small-business-email-marketing/ (Accessed April 18, 2014)

More information and tips on email marketing: Constant Contact and MailChimp

Chapter 10. Getting Repeat Business and Referrals

"Profit in business comes from repeat customers,
customers that boast about your project or service,
and that bring friends with them."
— W. Edwards Deming

If you change "customers" to "clients" and "friends" to "colleagues," Deming's quote concisely sums up the ultimate goal of marketing a freelance writing business. The simplest and least expensive way to market your services is to focus on two things:

1. Repeat business from satisfied clients, and
2. Referrals from them, the people they know, and your colleagues.

Nearly all of my new business these days comes from repeat business and referrals. I market actively only when I want to explore working with a new type of client or doing a new type of writing.

TIP
Maximize your marketing results by focusing on the vital few.

Focus on the Vital Few
Twenty percent of something is always responsible for 80% of the results, according to the 80/20 Rule. Quality management pioneer Dr. Joseph Juran calls this the "vital few and trivial many." In marketing, about 20 percent of your clients (the vital few) will produce 80 percent of your work and income. Focus your marketing efforts on them.

Keep Clients Coming Back for More

Most clients want to build strong, ongoing relationships with freelance writers that they can work with over the long term. It's easier, more efficient and more economical to work with writers who have done a good job in the past than to try to find new writers. I've been working with one of my clients since 1998 and another since 1999.

Building Long-Term Relationships with Clients

- Do a great job on every project.
- Do more than you're asked to do.
- Become a trusted advisor.
- Finish on time (or earlier) and on (or under) budget.
- Communicate often and effectively.
- Be likeable.
- Be professional.

Do More Than Expected

Keep current clients coming back for more by doing more than expected. For example, a patient told me in an interview about his experiences as a soldier on skis during World War II. I could have just written what he told me, but I did some Web research and found some great details about the unit he served in. I used this as a creative and interesting lead for the story. For another client, I developed a status update document to help me stay on track with the project. I sent this to the client weekly so she could see what I had accomplished and have an early warning about any issues (e.g., arranging interviews or getting source approvals).

Doing the Minimum Shows

Clients know when a writer does the minimum on a project. As a reviewer for one of my clients, I see what other writers turn in. Some always do a great job and are a pleasure to work with. Others do only what they think they have to do to get by. It's frustrating to work with these "minimalists" because they miss things they shouldn't and often do a poor job on revisions.

As a client myself (when I've subcontracted work to other writers), I've also seen differences in effort and quality. There are a few writers I'll call every time I have work to subcontract and others I'd never work with again.

Stay on Deadline and on Budget, and Communicate Clearly and Often

Complete the work on time and on budget. If you're going to be late, let the client know as early as possible. But this should only happen for professional reasons beyond your control, such as waiting for information from the client or for an interview with someone who's on vacation, or for personal emergencies (e.g., a family member is rushed to the hospital). Include the reason and next steps to resolve the problem.

Also let the client know about any other problems with a project. For projects that take more than a few weeks, send the client updates on your progress.

Acknowledge every question or request from a client promptly, even if you don't have the answer. It's far better, and more professional, to say, "I'll get back to you about this tomorrow," than to leave the client waiting for a response. When a client sends you something, acknowledge that you received it. You never want a client to have to email or call you again to see if you got a request, background materials, an article for revision, etc.

Make the Client's Life Easier

Clients like to work with people they like. Go out of your way to make your work together a pleasant experience. Position yourself as a trusted advisor. Suggest ways to improve the project (without raising the cost to the client). Send the client links to relevant articles or information. All of these things make the client's life easier and build your reputation as a professional who is easy to work with.

Getting Repeat Business

Often, clients will simply give you more work once you've done a good job on a project. But you can also let them know you're interesting in doing more work with them. When you finish a project, let the client know that you enjoyed working on it and would love to work with the client again. If there are other types of work you'd like to do for the client (which you know they do from your market research), this is a perfect opportunity to mention that you also write, for example, CME or Web content, or whatever you're interested in doing.

As you're working together, look for unmet needs. For example, I started out just writing newsletter articles for one client. When she mentioned that she wanted to start a new newsletter for another hospital service line, I said I'd done this before and would be glad to help her. I ended up developing the content ideas, working with the designer and then writing every issue. Over the next few years, I started four more newsletters for this client.

Another client hired me to write a quarterly newsletter for referring physicians. After we had done a few issues together and I knew she was satisfied with my work, I mentioned that I also love to write for consumers and patients and would be happy to help her out if she needed freelance help with this. She started assigning me stories for a consumer magazine that I now write for regularly.

Get More Referrals

Clients prefer to do business with people they know—or people recommended by people they know—than with strangers. A client will be more comfortable hiring a writer recommended by a colleague than just picking names out of the AMWA Freelance Directory or LinkedIn. These are important marketing tools, but referrals are more effective.

Letting Satisfied Clients Market Your Services

TIP: Focus on always doing great work and the referrals will come.

Satisfied clients are your best source of referrals. If you do a great job, become a trusted resource and make life easier for clients, they'll refer you when they know of someone else who's looking for a freelance medical writer. I actually had a client say to me, "I hope you don't mind, but I referred a colleague to you." Here are some of my referral stories:

- Several people I worked with at one organization hired me again when they moved to other organizations.
- A doctor I interviewed for a hospital newsletter story told the marketing director of her practice about me. The marketing director hired me to write Web content.
- A marketing director for whom I wrote newsletters referred me to her organization's website director, and I wrote Web content for him.
- A client referred me to the marketing folks at an affiliate organization.

Getting referrals takes time, so be patient. Focus on doing great work, and the referrals will come.

Building Your AMWA Network

AMWA members who know you are another great source of referrals. Giving someone a referral can enhance or damage the reputation of the person who makes the referral. That's why it's important to refer work only to people you know will do good work.

The people I've referred to freelance writing opportunities include my co-chair on an AMWA-DVC committee after we worked together for about a year and a colleague I met at an AMWA annual conference after we corresponded for a while and she served on a panel I organized for another annual conference. The referrals I've received include a colleague who served with me on my chapter's board and a colleague who participated in a conference I was organizing.

The common thread in referrals is knowledge about the person and trust in his or her abilities. Never ask people you've just met for referrals. Several people have done this to me, which puts them at the top of my list of people never to refer for anything.

Building a Referral Network

TIP:
Become a valued resource to others by matching clients and writers.

When someone does give you a referral, send a card or, if the referral works out, a gift (e.g., a gift certificate to Amazon). People appreciate this, and will be more likely to refer work to you again in the future.

If a potential client contacts you about work you don't do or don't have time for, offer to find another writer who might meet their needs. You'll be helping the client solve his or her immediate needs and positioning yourself as someone the client wants to work with in the future (or will refer to others if your writing and the client's work don't match at all). The person to whom you refer will also see you as a valued resource, and be more likely to refer opportunities to you in the future.

Collaborating with Other Freelance Writers

There's plenty of freelance medical writing work to go around. Collaboration always beats competition. Develop your own formal referral network of other freelance writers who do similar and different types of work than you do. While there may be some competition between you and writers who do similar work, they are more likely than other writers to know of work that's right for you. Also, if they can't take on new work, they'll need someone they can refer clients to.

Collaborating with people who do different types of work allows you to provide referrals when you're asked about work you don't do, thus, expanding your network of clients and freelance medical writers who may refer work to you in the future. Also, a prospective client will be more likely to contact you again in the future, for a project that's right for you, if you've been helpful in the past (i.e., you helped them find a writer for another project).

The idea of the referral network is to let other freelance writers know about the type of work you do and would like to do and find out what they do and would like to do. Develop a referral network form, and send your completed form and a blank form when you invite someone to join your referral network. Put this in a referral network folder in your computer so the forms are always handy when you hear of someone looking for a freelance medical writer.

Sample Referral Network Form Template

Who I Am: Name, company name, email, phone number(s) and website

What I Do: Brief summary (less than 50 words)

My Ideal Clients: (Types of organization you'd most like to work with, e.g., medical communications companies, hospitals or pharmaceutical companies)

Other Types of Clients I Work With: (Types of organizations you work with)

Types of Writing I'm Most Interested In: (Include media, such as journal articles, slide decks or newsletter articles, and therapeutic areas, such as diabetes and oncology)

Other Types of Writing I Do: (Include media, such as journal articles, slide decks or newsletter articles, and therapeutic areas, such as diabetes and oncology)

Special Skills: (Other skills that a client might need, e.g., project management or strategic communications)

Notes: (To be added after getting the form back from the writer. Include how and when you met, your initial thoughts about the person and comments based on research you've done, such as visiting the writer's website.)

Before inviting people you don't know very well to your formal referral network, like people you meet at the AMWA annual conference or through a LinkedIn discussion, vet them. Visit their websites, LinkedIn pages and AMWA Freelance Directory listings. Make sure their websites and profiles are professional and you would be proud to refer work to them. Try to build relationships with people you don't know really well before referring work to them.

Resources

ARTICLES

Perry Marshall, "The 80/20 Rule of Sales: How to Find Your Best Customers." www.entrepreneur.com/article/229294 (Accessed April 8, 2014)

Robert Moskowitz, "How to Get Repeat Business From Your Clients." blog.intuit.com/marketing/how-to-get-repeat-business-from-your-clients (Accessed April 8, 2014)

BONUS MATERIAL

Bonus #1: Quick-Start Marketing Guide

"Your attitude, not your aptitude, will determine your altitude."
—Zig Ziglar

Start marketing your freelance medical writing business in days with some market research and a few easy, effective marketing tools.

High-Impact, Low- or No-Cost Marketing Tools

- Elevator pitch
- Business card and email signature
- LinkedIn
- AMWA Freelance Directory
- Networking

Explore Your Options Through Market Research

Learn about the many freelance medical writing opportunities and the many types of clients you might work for through market research. AMWA makes it easy to do this online and in person.

As you do your market research, take notes about:

- Types of clients you'd like to work with
- Specific organizations you'd like to work with
- Therapeutic areas you'd like to work in.

Learn About the Marketplace Through AMWA

Some Web-based resources:
- Toolkit for New Medical Writers (see the section on freelance medical writing)
- Freelance Directory (read the profiles of freelance medical writers)

Face-to-face networking with other freelance medical writers and potential clients:
- AMWA annual conference
- AMWA Delaware Valley Chapter freelance conference
- Chapter meetings and conferences

Virtual networking with other freelance medical writers and potential clients:
- AMWA LinkedIn groups
- AMWA community forums

Understand What Clients Want

Clients of freelance medical writers have a strong interest in our services. They need our help to succeed.

What Clients Want (Generally)

- Excellent writing skills and the ability to meet deadlines (the keys to repeat business)
- Experience (in medical writing, the therapeutic area and the type of writing)
- Specific degree(s)
- Excellent communication skills
- Flexibility, accessibility and responsiveness
- Ability to take ownership of the project

Target Your Services

Understanding the freelance medical writing marketplace—and your place in it—will help you target and market your services appropriately and build long-term, win-win relationships with clients.

High-Impact, Low- or No-Cost Marketing Tools

Some of the best marketing tools for freelance medical writers—elevator pitch, business card, email signature, LinkedIn, AMWA Freelance Directory and networking—are free or low-cost. You can put them all to work for you in a few days. A great website is another essential marketing tool for freelance medical writers, but developing this takes time, effort and money. It's okay to make this part of your phase two marketing.

Your Elevator Pitch

When you meet people in person for the first time, your elevator pitch (also called elevator speech) is a key tool for creating a positive first impression. What will you say so that people understand—in 60 seconds or less—what you do? Your elevator pitch should cover what you can do for clients and how you can solve their problems (the benefits or results of your work).

Think about your elevator pitch before you head out the door. Write down your ideas and say them aloud to see how they sound. Refine your ideas until you've got a concise, compelling way to introduce yourself. Practice your elevator pitch, because using it won't feel natural.

Your Business Card

A great business card is a small but powerful ad for your business. Done right, it will help colleagues and potential clients remember you, especially when they get back to the office with a stack of business cards. Done wrong, it will mark you as unprofessional, as will not having a business card at all.

Business cards are the only quick-start marketing tool that you have to order, but if you're willing to pay extra, you can get them printed fast. You can get business cards in one day at Staples, for example, and Vistaprint has three-day shipping.

Attributes of a Great Business Card

- Clear, concise information
- Clean, legible, professional design
- Branded (after you've developed your brand)
- Professionally printed

Information to include:
- Your name
- Company name (if you have one now)
- Tagline (if you have one now) or a brief description of your services (if your company name doesn't clearly say what you do)
- Logo (if you have one now)
- Business phone number
- Email address
- Website (if you have one now)

Optional information:
- Mailing address
- LinkedIn address

Design and Printing

Your business card design should be clean and simple so people can easily see who you are, what you do and how to contact you. Make the most important information most prominent.

For your first business cards, you can use templates available through Web-based services like Vistaprint (vistaprint.com) or Staples (Staples.com) to design and then print your business cards professionally at reasonable prices. Later, after you've developed your brand and hired a designer for your business card, website and other marketing materials, go back and print new business cards. If you've already had your business card professionally designed, you can upload it to these services for printing.

> **TIP:**
> Always carry a few business cards. You could meet a potential client anywhere at any time.

Email Signature

Your email signature is another easy and mighty, but often neglected, marketing tool. At a minimum, include:

- Your name
- A brief description of your services
- Your business phone number and email
- Your LinkedIn address.

If you have a company name, tagline, logo, website or any of these, include them too.

Online Profiles: LinkedIn and AMWA Freelance Directory

Next, develop compelling profiles for LinkedIn and the AMWA Freelance Directory. With 250 million members (as of April 2014), LinkedIn is the world's largest professional network. Clients can search the AWMA Freelance Directory for free. At $75 a year for an ad (in 2014), it's a real bargain. I've covered LinkedIn first because you can be proactive on LinkedIn and seek out opportunities, whereas with the AMWA Freelance Directory, clients have to find you.

Crafting Persuasive Profiles

Write to your target audience and focus on the benefits you provide in both your LinkedIn and AMWA Freelance Directory profiles. Much of the content will be the same.

Elements of Persuasive Profiles

Content:

- Scintillating summary or description with an enticing headline or first sentence, benefits to your target audience, and clear, simple description of who you are and what you do
- Summary of experience, services and therapeutic areas
- More details on experience
- Education
- Relevant honors and awards
- Clear call to action (e.g., call or email, visit my website, connect on LinkedIn, or any combination of these)
- Five strategic keywords or phrases used throughout your profile
- Links to your website, writing samples or both

Format:

- Headlines and subheads
- Short, action-oriented sentences
- Short paragraphs
- Bulleted lists

Use key messages from your elevator pitch, the services you've decided to offer and the therapeutic areas you work in to craft your profiles.

> **TIP:**
> Study LinkedIn and Freelance Directory profiles of other freelance writers for good ideas.

There are some differences in the formats of LinkedIn and the Freelance Directory that affect what you'll say and how your profile will look. For example, LinkedIn lets you post a photo, while the Freelance Directory doesn't. But the Freelance Directory is easier to format than a LinkedIn profile and lets you do more with font size. LinkedIn also has specific sections where you enter your information (e.g., summary, experience, publications, skills and endorsements, organizations and education). In the Freelance Directory description you can include any information you'd like to, and you can create your own sections.

Test your LinkedIn and AMWA Freelance Directory profiles as soon as you've finalized them to make sure they read well and look right.

LinkedIn

A LinkedIn profile starts with your name and below that, a headline. Write a compelling headline based on your elevator speech and including the benefits clients get when they hire you. To the left of this is a space for a photo. Invest in a professional headshot, which you can also use on your website. Include your contact information so people who view your profile can get in touch with you.

> **TIP:**
> Also include keywords after advice for contacting you.

Learn more about using LinkedIn after you've developed your profile in the section on networking.

AMWA Freelance Directory

Most clients search for specific therapeutic areas (using the keywords search boxes) when using the Freelance Directory. Be sure and include your areas of expertise. The search screen also allows clients to search by service types and media types (by selecting categories), as well as last name, city and state, degree and years of experience (0-5, 6-10, 11-15, 16-20, 21-25, and 26+). Since you can create your own sections, consider including testimonials from satisfied clients.

Networking

Who you know—a.k.a. your network—can be one of the most important factors in landing clients. Continually grow your network in person and using social media. Focus on establishing your trustworthiness, competence and reliability. Always:

- Give more than you take
- Be a useful resource to others
- Cultivate lasting and meaningful relationships with key people.

Essential Networking Tools

- Social networking through LinkedIn
- In-person networking through AMWA and other groups
- Volunteering for AMWA and other groups

Give More, Take Less

TIP:
Share knowledge, make introductions and mentor others

Helping others without expecting anything in return—or giving more than you take—is the best way to build a solid network. Sharing relevant information and resources, and connecting people, boosts credibility and builds trust. The people you help will remember you when they have a freelance opportunity or something else to share. It's also easier to ask someone for help in the future if you've helped her or him in the past.

People who give their time to others without expecting anything in return are more successful than people who don't do this, according to Adam Grant, a management professor at the University of Pennsylvania. Grant is the author of the best-selling book "Give and Take."

Focus on Key Contacts: Your Ecosystem

> **TIP:**
> Keep a spreadsheet of people you'd like to cultivate and your contacts with them. Review it regularly.

Networking, like all marketing, should be strategic. While you should be nice and helpful to everyone you meet (virtually or in person), focus most of your networking efforts on cultivating mutually beneficial relationships with key people. Freelance medical writers Jeanne McAdara-Berkowitz and Christine Welniak call this an ecosystem, defined as "a system of interconnecting and interacting parts" (Dictionary.com).

You and the people in your ecosystem will share many things, including:

- Information
- Resources
- Advice
- Experiences, good and bad
- Solutions to problems
- Referrals to clients.

When you meet someone you think might become part of your ecosystem, stay in touch and cultivate the relationship.

Ways to Stay in Touch

- Congratulate and compliment colleagues on professional achievements
- Comment on colleagues' work and activities (e.g., e-newsletter, blog posting or new writing sample)
- Send links to relevant articles or resources
- Notify colleagues about events they may want to attend
- Share freelance opportunities you hear about
- Send cards (holiday, birthday, thank-you, etc.)
- Get together at the AMWA annual conference
- Meet for coffee or a meal in person if you live close enough

Stay in touch with the people in your ecosystem at least two or three times a year by email, phone, mail, in person or a combination of these methods.

Meet the Right People Face-to-Face

AMWA—the #1 networking source for freelance medical writers—is made up of friendly, helpful people. Meet other medical writers, including freelancers like you, people who work for organizations, and potential clients, by:

- Attending the annual conference
- Attending the annual AMWA Delaware Valley Chapter freelance conference
- Attending events in your local chapter
- Participating in AMWA LinkedIn groups and AMWA community forums.

Strategic In-Person Networking

- Bring business cards (a lot) and your elevator pitch
- Set a goal, like having good conversations with two people
- Listen for ways you can help the other person (by making introductions and sharing information and resources)
- Ask people questions about themselves
- Be pleasant and professional
- Don't spend too much time with one person

Follow up with the people you'd like to stay in touch with. An invitation to join your LinkedIn network or an email to say "nice to meet you" is an easy way to do this. Emailing with useful information or resources is even better (e.g., a link to an article related to work the person is doing, or a resource on something you discussed). Include details of how and where you met.

> **TIP:**
> Make notes on the back of business cards to help you remember each person.

The Power of Volunteering

Cultivating relationships that are strong enough for people to trust you and know you're competent requires more than casual interaction. The best way to do this is to become an AMWA volunteer. National AMWA and its chapters both have many interesting volunteer opportunities. Often, you'll meet—and have a chance to impress—AMWA leaders.

Connect with Others

Some of my thoughts on LinkedIn follow, but I'm no expert. Donna Serdula is, so see her LinkedIn Makeover resources at the end of this guide for how to really work LinkedIn.

Build Your LinkedIn Network

After writing a great profile, connect with others to start building your LinkedIn network. If you want people to find you, you need to be part of their network.

Your LinkedIn Network

A LinkedIn network is made up of:

- **First-degree connections**: People who invite you to be part of their network or accept your invitation to be part of your network.
- **Second-degree connections**: People who are connected to your first-degree connections. You can invite them to connect with you.
- **Third-degree connections**: People who are connected to your second-degree connections. You can connect with them, but you may need to ask your second-degree connection for an introduction (depending on how the person has set up his or her account).
- **Members of your LinkedIn groups:** You can contact fellow group members by sending a message on LinkedIn or participating in discussions.

I only connect with people I know. My connections are a reflection on me, and I don't want to introduce someone I don't know well to another connection. LinkedIn also recommends only making first-degree connections with people you know and trust. Some people, including Serdula, believe it's better to connect with almost anyone to build your network and appear more often in search results. But if too many people respond to an invitation to connect with "I don't know" or "Report as spam," LinkedIn will restrict or terminate your account.

When you invite people to join your network, take a few seconds to write something interesting, or at least personal (e.g., about how you know each other.) Don't use the default "I'd like to add you to my professional network on LinkedIn."

Getting Noticed

Use LinkedIn actively and attract positive attention through updates and groups. Updates are short (600 characters maximum) notes that keep your connections thinking about you through periodic network updates LinkedIn sends out. The top of your homepage, next to your photo, has a "Share an update" bar where you can share:

- Expert advice
- Links to interesting news
- Links to interesting articles
- Upcoming events
- Questions and requests
- Examples of your work, if relevant and interesting to your connections
- More.

You can include Web links and attach files to updates.

TIP:
Get ideas for your updates from the updates of your connections, which appear on your home page.

Highlighting Expertise and Building Relationships through Groups

People who participate in groups get four times as many profile views as people who don't, says LinkedIn. Groups let you share your expertise and build relationships.

Good groups for freelance medical writers include AMWA, Medical Marketing & Communications Group, Drug Information

Association, the Freelance Writers Connection, and alumni groups. Ways to find other groups include:

- Checking out the groups potential clients belong to (see Groups near the bottom of their profiles)
- Checking out the groups other freelance medical writers belong to (see Groups near the bottom of their profiles)
- Taking suggestions from LinkedIn
- Doing a general search for groups (under the Interests tab at the top).

When you comment or start a discussion, your name and the headline from your LinkedIn profile appears above the comment or just below the headline of your discussion topic.

> **TIP:**
> Get ideas for starting discussions from discussions in your groups.

Once you've gotten the feel of a group, start discussions yourself. Focus on topics of relevance and interest to group members.

Other Social Networks

Explore other social networks, including AMWA community forums, which might be useful to you.

Keep on Marketing

Quick-start marketing is only the beginning of your marketing journey. As Beverly Sills said, "There are no shortcuts to any place worth going." This guide is a way to start marketing your freelance writing business quickly. It's not a way to avoid developing your brand, marketing plan and website. Nor is it a substitute for investing the time, work and money necessary to become a mighty marketer. After you've developed the high-impact, low- or no-cost marketing tools, continue your marketing journey by reading the rest of this book.

Get Repeat Business and Referrals

The ultimate goal of marketing your freelance writing business is to get:

- Repeat business from satisfied clients
- Referrals for new business from them, the people they know and your colleagues.

Mighty marketers get lots of repeat business and lots of referrals. If you're smart enough to be a freelance medical writer, you're smart enough to become a mighty marketer. Enjoy the marketing journey!

Quick-Start Marketing Resources

MARKET RESEARCH AND NETWORKING

American Medical Writers Association (AMWA)

AMWA (National organization):

www.amwa.org (Some information is only available to members)

Toolkit for New Medical Writers: Includes an overview of medical writing, including types of employers and types of work, with a section on freelance medical writing.

Freelance Directory: By searching the Freelance Directory, you can learn more about what other freelance medical writers do and how they market themselves.

About Medical Communication: Resources about medical communication, including a PowerPoint presentation.

AMWA community forums: Learn about medical writing and what AMWA members are doing through forums like Tools and Resources, Freelance, Regulatory Writing and CME.

Education tab: Annual conference information.

AMWA-Delaware Valley Chapter
(www.amwa-dvc.org)
> Annual freelance conference (held every spring; see Upcoming Events a few months before).
> *Delawriter* newsletter, with articles about many aspects of medical writing, including freelancing

BUSINESS CARDS

John Williams. "The ABCs of Business Cards." Entrepreneur. http://www.entrepreneur.com/article/159468 (Accessed March 29, 2014)

ONLINE PRINTER

Vistaprint: www.vistaprint.com: An economical and easy way to print business cards and other marketing materials.

LINKEDIN

Donna Serdula, "The LinkedIn Makeover Book: Professional Secrets to a POWERFUL LinkedIn Profile," Second edition, 2013: www.linkedin-makeover.com/book (Accessed May 12, 2014)

Free LinkedIn Makeover resources: http://www.linkedin-makeover.com/linkedin-resources/ (Accessed May 12, 2014)

NETWORKING

Adam Grant, "Give and Take," Penguin Books, 2013. www.giveandtake.com/Home/Book.

GENERAL MARKETING

Jay Conrad Levinson and Jeannie Levinson. "Guerrilla Marketing Field Guide: 30 Powerful Maneuvers for Non-Stop Momentum and Results," Entrepreneur Press 2013.

Bonus #2: Mighty Marketing Worksheets, Templates and Tools

"The essence of strategy is choosing what not to do."
— Michael Porter

Opportunity in freelance medical writing abounds, but you have to go out and find it. Focus your marketing and make the best use of your limited time and money with these worksheets, templates and tools. This will take some time and effort, but it's an investment in your business that will pay off and make future marketing much easier.

Define Your Services and Target Markets

Set marketing priorities for your services and therapeutic areas and begin to identify specific clients to target. These worksheets focus on four priorities at each level, but this isn't a magic number. It's okay to have more (but not too many more) or less in each category.

Worksheet: Priority Services

#1 Priority Services
Experience and enthusiasm: Types of medical writing I currently do (or have done) and am eager to pursue.

Service #1 _____

Service #2 _____

Service #3 _____

Service #4 _____

#2 Priority Services

Experience but no enthusiasm: Types of medical writing I do (or have done) but am **not** eager to pursue.

Service #5 _____

Service #6_____

Service #7_____

Service #8_____

#3 Priority Services

Enthusiasm but no experience: Types of medical writing I really want to do and think I can do.

Service #9 _____

Service #10_____

Service #11_____

Service #12_____

If you're an experienced, stable freelance medical writer looking to market more aggressively, make this your second priority and skip looking for work you've done but don't want to do more of.

Worksheet: Priority Therapeutic Areas

#1 Priority Therapeutic Areas

Experience and enthusiasm: Therapeutic areas I've worked in and am eager to pursue.

Area #1 _____

Area #2 _____

Area #3 _____

Area #4 _____

#2 Priority Therapeutic Areas

Experience but no enthusiasm: Therapeutic areas I work (or have worked) in but am **not** eager to pursue.

Area #5 _____

Area #6 _____

Area #7 _____

Area #8 _____

#3 Priority Therapeutic Areas

Enthusiasm but no experience: Therapeutic areas I really want to work in and think I can do.

Area #9 _____

Area #10 _____

Area #11 _____

Area #12 _____

Worksheet: Priority Clients

If you're not yet established, cast a wide net. If you're an experienced freelance medical writer, you can target your market more strategically.

#1 Priority Clients

Experience and enthusiasm: The type of clients I've worked with and would like to pursue.

Type of client #1_____

Type of client #2_____

Type of client #3_____

Type of client #4_____

Specific clients I've identified so far (put this in a Word document and include as much information as you have so far):
> Potential client:
> Contact:
> Contact's title:
> Email address and phone number:
> Address:
> Website:

Repeat for each potential client.

#2 Priority Clients

Experience but no enthusiasm: Types of clients I've worked with but am **not** eager to pursue.

Type of client #5 _____

Type of client #6_____

Type of client #7_____

Type of client #8_____

Specific clients I've identified so far (create a Word document):
> Potential client:
> Contact:
> Contact's title:
> Email address and phone number:
> Address:
> Website:

Repeat for each potential client.

#3 Priority Clients

Enthusiasm but no experience: Types of clients I really want to work with.

Type of client #9 _____

Type of client #10_____

Type of client #11_____

Type of client #12_____

Specific clients I've identified so far (create a Word document):

Potential client:
Contact:
Contact's title:
Email address and phone number:
Address:
Website:

Repeat for each potential client.

Set Your Marketing Goals

Make your goals challenging, but achievable and easy to measure. Your 12-month goal should be concrete, while your five-year goal will be broader and more abstract. Your two-year goal will be somewhere in between.

My marketing goal for the next 12 months (include the end month and year) is to:

_____

_____

My marketing goal for the next two years (include the end month and year) is to:

_____

_____

My marketing goal for the next five years (include the end month and year) is to:

_____

_____

Choose Your Tools

Choosing the marketing tools you'll use, at least the initial tools, is easy. I've listed the #1 priority tools (the high-impact, low- or no-cost marketing tools) for you. Add website development as soon as you can and consider other marketing tools later.

Worksheet: Tools

#1 Priority Tools

Tool #1: Elevator pitch
Tool #2: Business card and email signature
Tool #3: LinkedIn
Tool #4: AMWA Freelance Directory
Tool #5: Networking

#2 Priority Tools

Tool #6: Website

#3 Priority Tools

Choose from:
- Direct mail
- Email marketing
- Cards and gifts for clients
- Cards for prospects and colleagues
- Printed marketing materials
- Volunteering for AMWA and other organizations or groups
- Publishing
- Speaking and teaching

Tool #7: _____

Tool #8 _____

Tool # 9 _____

Tool # 10 _____

Tool # 11 _____

Tool # 12 _____

Annual Marketing Calendar

Stay on track with an annual marketing calendar, organized by quarters (or months if you really want to be a mighty marketer). Complete each action item by the deadline, as if you were working for a client. Marketing actions that take a long time, like developing a website, can be continued over two or more quarters. Review your marketing actions at least twice a month, or ideally weekly.

Annual Marketing Calendar Template

First quarter:

> Review of marketing actions: (e.g., every Friday)
> Review of marketing plan: (e.g., last Friday of the quarter)

> Action item #1:
> Deadline:
> Date completed:
> Cost:

> Action item #2:
> Deadline:
> Date completed:
> Cost:

Repeat for every action item.

Review the sample marketing actions for a freelance medical writing business below, and then develop your marketing calendar. Update it as needed.

Sample Marketing Actions: Year #1

(First quarter by month and the rest by quarter)

First quarter:

January
> Every Friday afternoon: Review marketing actions
> Action item #1: Develop elevator pitch
> Action item #2: Develop and print initial business card
> Action item #3: Develop email signature

Action item #4: Develop and post LinkedIn profile

Action item #5: Develop and post AMWA Freelance Directory profile

February

Every Friday afternoon: Review marketing actions

Action item #1: Develop your brand

Action item #2: Post LinkedIn update weekly

Action item #3: Start connecting with people on LinkedIn

Action item #4: Start reading AMWA online communities

Action item #5: Start reading AMWA LinkedIn group discussions

Action item #6: Attend AMWA local chapter event

March

Every Friday afternoon: Review marketing actions

Last Friday: Review marketing plan and update as needed

Action item #1: Post LinkedIn update weekly

Action item #2: Connect with x new people on LinkedIn

Action item #3: Continue research to develop prospect lists

Action item #4: Participate in AMWA LinkedIn group discussions

Action item #5: Participate in AMWA online communities

Action item #6: Volunteer for AMWA

Action item #7: Attend AMWA local chapter event

Second through fourth quarters:

Continue routine marketing efforts (e.g., posting LinkedIn updates, connecting with new people on LinkedIn and participating in the AMWA LinkedIn groups). Also continue weekly review of marketing actions and quarterly review of your marketing plan. Add new marketing actions.

Second quarter:

> Action item #1: Hire a designer to implement your brand
>
> Action item #2: Reprint your business cards with your brand
>
> Action item #3: Start developing content for your website

Third quarter:

> Action item #1: Continue developing content for your website
>
> Action item #2: Continue volunteer work for AMWA
>
> Action item #3: Attend the AMWA annual conference (networking)

Fourth quarter:

> Action item #1: Hire a web designer to develop your website
>
> Action item #2: Attend the AMWA annual conference
>
> Action item #3: Send holiday cards to clients, prospects and colleagues
>
> Action item #4: Update marketing plan for next year

Marketing Actions: Year #2 and Beyond

By your second year in business, you'll have learned about the medical writing marketplace and developed all of the basic marketing tools. If you haven't developed your website yet, make that a priority now. Begin refining your marketing and adding other effective marketing tools to your marketing plan and calendar, like:

- More focused networking and reputation building (e.g., develop a network of key contacts, get more involved as an volunteer for AMWA and other relevant groups)
- Direct mail or email
- Other printed marketing materials (e.g., postcards, thank-you cards, and notes)
- Publishing (e.g., AMWA Journal, e-zines, publications and websites)
- Speaking and teaching (e.g., roundtables, presentations and courses for AMWA, presentations and teaching for other groups).

Set Aside a Budget

Invest enough money to develop high-quality marketing materials. For the first year in business, or the first year you rev up your marketing, I'd recommend about $5,000-$8,000 if you develop your website and attend the AMWA annual conference and about $2,000 if you do neither of these things. If you don't develop your website until the next year, budget for it then (roughly $1,000-$3,000). (Estimated costs are as of 2014.)

Some costs are fixed or standard, such as AMWA membership, freelance directory, and annual conference; and printing business cards and other marketing materials. Other costs, such as design services (print and web), vary by geographic region and vendor.

My marketing budget for the next 12 months
(include the end month and year) is:
$ _____.

Track your marketing expenses with a simple list, and includes notes to guide future marketing (e.g., whether you liked the vendor and any other vendors you may have heard about and might want to use in the future). When you review your marketing over time, add notes about whether a marketing tool worked for you. For example:

Expense: 500 business cards
Vendor: Vistaprint
Amount: $32
Date: 6/8/14
Notes: Great vendor. Reasonable prices and fast turnaround.

Marketing Expenses Template

Template
Expense: (marketing tool)
Vendor:
Amount:
Date:
Notes:

Repeat for all marketing expenses.

Bonus #3: Awesome Marketing Copy and Content Checklist

"Easy reading is damn hard writing."
— Nathaniel Hawthorne

Before you finalize marketing copy (for print) and content (for the Web), use this checklist to make sure it will be awesome. If you can answer "yes" to all of these questions, you'll capture—and keep—the attention of your target audiences.

Key Messages
- ☐ Do I convey key messages fast?
- ☐ Do I focus on the benefits to my target audience?
- ☐ Is my writing clear and concise?
- ☐ Am I using key messages from my branding?

Tone
- ☐ Do I use the right tone (informal, for most marketing copy and content)?
- ☐ Do I write in the active voice?
- ☐ Do I come across as credible and confident?

Writing
- ☐ Do I use attention-grabbing headlines and subheads?
- ☐ Are sentences simple?
- ☐ Are paragraphs short?
- ☐ Do I use lots of verbs?
- ☐ Do I use bulleted lists?
- ☐ Do I have a call to action?
- ☐ Is my writing free of mistakes (spelling, grammar, etc.)?

Bonus #4: Top 10 Ways to Become a Mighty Marketer

"If you're smart enough to be a freelance medical writer, you're smart enough to be a mighty marketer."
—Lori De Milto

This Top 10 list is presented in reverse priority order, in keeping with David Letterman's Top 10 lists.

10. **Be informed.** Target and market your services appropriately, and build win-win relationships with clients, by learning about the medical writing marketplace. Match your interests, experience and capabilities with the needs of prospective clients.

9. **Be inspired.** Good marketing ideas are everywhere, once you open your mind to them. Pay attention to ads on websites and television, the email marketing that stores and organizations send you, direct mail you get at home, marketing by other freelance writers—and everything around you.

8. **Partner with experts**. You don't have to—and shouldn't—market alone. Partner with experts for logo development, print design, website design and other things outside your areas of expertise.

7. **Collaborate with other freelance medical writers.** There's plenty of interesting work for everyone. We can all learn from each other and share resources and opportunities. Collaboration always beats competition.

6. **Develop high-impact, low- or no-cost marketing tools—and a website**. Some of the best marketing tools for freelance medical writers—elevator speech, business card, email signature, LinkedIn, AMWA Freelance Directory and networking—are free

or low-cost. A great website is another essential (but unfortunately, not low-cost) marketing tool for freelance medical writers.

5. Plan and prioritize. Develop a plan to make the most of your marketing time and money. Start with high-impact, low-effort tools. Focus on the tools most likely to work for you.

4. Give more than you take. Good things come to people who help others without expecting anything in return. Sharing relevant information and resources, connecting people and giving in other ways boosts your credibility and builds trust. People who do these things are more successful than those who don't.

3. Join and get actively involved in AMWA. Make key contacts with potential clients and other freelance medical writers and learn about medical writing through AWMA. Build your reputation as a credible, trustworthy colleague by volunteering.

2. Invest in marketing. Marketing a business—and freelance medical writing is a business—takes time and money. These are the seeds of your success; plant them right and your freelance medical writing business will bloom.

1. Do great work—always. Focus on doing great work and repeat business and referrals will come. Always do more than expected. Complete the work on time and on budget. Become a trusted advisor to clients, and communicate often and effectively.

Bonus #5: Top 10 Mighty Marketing Resources

"A person who never made a mistake never tried anything new."
—Albert Einstein

This Top 10 list is presented in reverse priority order, in keeping with David Letterman's Top 10 lists.

10. Email marketing services and tips: Constant Contact (constantcontact.com) and MailChimp (mailchimp.com).

9. Web content: Janice (Ginny) Redish, "Letting Go of the Words: Writing Web Content that Works." Second edition. San Francisco, CA: Morgan Kauffmann Publishers, 2012. Available on Amazon.com.

8. General marketing: Catriona Mackay, "Effective Marketing in Easy Steps." United Kingdom: Easy Steps Limited, 2011. Available on Amazon.com.

7. General marketing: C.J. Hayden, "Get Clients Now! A 28-Day Marketing Program for Professionals, Consultants, and Coaches," 2013. Available on Amazon.com.

6. Networking: Adam Grant, "Give and Take." Penguin Books, 2013. www.giveandtake.com/Home/Book. Also available on Amazon.com.

5. Direct mail: Craig Simpson with Dan S. Kennedy, "The Direct Mail Solution: A Business Owner's Guide to Building a Lead-Generating, Sales-Driving, Money-Making Direct-Mail Campaign." Entrepreneur Media, 2014. Available on Amazon.com.

4. General marketing: Jay Conrad Levinson and Jeannie Levinson, "Guerrilla Marketing Field Guide: 30 Powerful Maneuvers for Non-Stop Momentum and Results." Entrepreneur Press 2013. Available on Amazon.com.

3. Online printer: Vistaprint (www.vistaprint.com): An economical and easy way to print business cards and other marketing materials.

2. LinkedIn: Donna Serdula, "The LinkedIn Makeover Book: Professional Secrets to a POWERFUL LinkedIn Profile." Second edition, 2013 (www.linkedin-makeover.com/book) and Free LinkedIn Makeover resources (http://www.linkedin-makeover.com/linkedin-resources)

1. Targeted marketing for freelance medical writers:
American Medical Writers Association (AMWA)
AMWA (National organization):
www.amwa.org (Some information is only available to members)

> Toolkit for New Medical Writers: Includes an overview of medical writing, including types of employers and types of work, with a section on freelance medical writing

> Freelance Directory: By searching the Freelance Directory, you can learn more about what other freelance medical writers do and how they market themselves.

> About Medical Communication: Resources about medical communication, including a PowerPoint presentation.

> AMWA community forums: Learn about medical writing and what AMWA members are doing through forums like Tools and Resources, Freelance, Regulatory Writing and CME.

> Education tab: Annual conference information

AMWA-Delaware Valley Chapter

(www.amwa-dvc.org)

> Annual freelance conference (held every spring; see Upcoming Events in the winter for details).

> *Delawrite*r newsletter, with articles about many aspects of medical writing and summaries of presentations from past freelance conferences.

(All websites accurate as of May 2014)

CPSIA information can be obtained
at www.ICGtesting.com
Printed in the USA
BVHW01s0942110218
507805BV00006B/131/P